Instructor's Manual
and
Test Bank

to accompany

Reading
and
Study Skills

Seventh Edition

John Langan
Atlantic Cape Community College

Janet M. Goldstein

McGraw Hill

Boston   Burr Ridge, IL   Dubuque, IA   Madison, WI   New York   San Francisco   St. Louis
Bangkok   Bogotá   Caracas   Kuala Lumpur   Lisbon   London   Madrid   Mexico City
Milan   Montreal   New Delhi   Santiago   Seoul   Singapore   Sydney   Taipei   Toronto

McGraw-Hill Higher Education

A Division of The McGraw-Hill Companies

Instructor's Manual and Test Bank to accompany
READING AND STUDY SKILLS
John Langan and Janet M. Goldstein

2 3 4 5 6 7 8 9 0 HAM/HAM 0 9 8 7 6 5 4 3 2

ISBN 0-07-251839-1

www.mhhe.com

CONTENTS

Part Seven: Mastery Tests   54

Part Eight: Additional Learning Skills   64

30 ADDITIONAL MASTERY TESTS   67

SUGGESTED APPROACHES AND TECHNIQUES TO USE WITH THE BOOK

On the following pages, I describe briefly some approaches and techniques that have proved helpful while using the materials in the book.

1 I have found the following memory-building activity to be an invaluable one for the first class session: I ask the students to learn each other's first names. So that I do not get in the students' way while they are doing this, I leave the room for ten or fifteen minutes. When I return, I call for volunteers to introduce me, on a first-name basis, to all the people in the room.

Afterward, I ask students to describe *how* they went about mastering the first names of all the people in the class. They then have a chance to compare ideas with others on the memory processes that were used. They will probably discover that in most cases, the methods used to learn the names were similar. Additionally, they may realize for the first time that there *is* a definite process, or sequence of steps, involved in an act of memorization.

This activity has several benefits. Students learn each other's first names; they develop a sense of working together as a class; they surprise and please themselves with their success at the project; and they are prepared to learn the three basic steps in effective memorization described on pages 210–212.

2 I begin the semester with the chapter titled "Taking Classroom Notes" because students usually have one or more content courses along with their course or courses in developmental skills. They need to learn right away how to take effective notes in those courses.

One helpful device in teaching note-taking is to have instructors at your school videotape some "mini-lectures" in their disciplines, each lecture lasting about twenty minutes. The tapes can then be used for supervised practice in note-taking.

3 I do not proceed in an unvarying linear sequence. To combat lags in students' attention, I skip around freely and often provide practice in three or four skills within a three-hour class. The book's organization makes it easy to vary a class's activities.

4 I find that the chapter titled "Your Attitude: The Heart of the Matter" has more impact on students after the semester is about three weeks old. Students can look back to examine what they are or are not doing with their time in school.

I then save the chapter on "Learning Survival Strategies" for several weeks later. This chapter also encourages students to evaluate themselves as students, and it provides a boost—moral support and positive thinking—at a time when it may be needed.

5 As the directions for some of the activities in the book will show, I believe that students can often learn effectively by working with each other. Just as attention will decline if one skill is worked on unremittingly, so it will drop if all activities are carried out in one way. For some activities, students should work silently at their seats while the instructor goes around, observes their work in progress, and offers comments. (This is the best time to provide feedback—at the moment a student is involved in a task.) For other activities, students can be asked to work in pairs; and for yet other exercises, they can be divided into small groups of three or four. Such variety both sustains energy levels and enriches the learning process.

6   Skills work is hard work. It's not glamorous; trumpets don't sound, and the sky seldom turns technicolor. When students visibly flag, as they will if they are working hard, I sometimes announce a "milling-around break." Everyone stands up and mills around for a couple of minutes and gets the blood flowing again. Then we sit back down, noses to the grindstone again, a little fresher. I know an instructor who starts her classes with calisthenics; it may not be a bad idea.

7   I've found that grading students on most of their classroom and homework activities is an effective way of motivating them to put forth their best efforts. Accordingly, I may accumulate fifteen or more grades from a student in the course of a semester. When it is impractical both to grade many papers and to make individual comments on the papers, I note the most common areas of mistakes and discuss them in class rather than writing extensively on each paper.

In a typical class, where students with reasonable ability are making a reasonable effort, most of the grades should be good. The grades are invaluable because they show students that they are capable of success. Very often developmental students have received only negative feedback about their academic ability; positive reinforcement helps them blossom. The graded activities are also a constant check on whether a skill has been presented effectively in class. It is only natural at times that an instructor will miscalculate students' readiness to apply a particular skill. When this happens, a quiz can simply be marked with a check rather than with a number or letter grade.

8   Students' learning is often best measured by asking them to practice a skill, rather than by asking objective questions about the skill. In this regard, many of the activities in the book, particularly in the section on study skills, can be used as mastery tests. For example, Activities 4 to 6 on pages 63–69 can be used to measure students' skill at taking classroom notes.

At the same time, objective tests provide a traditional, detached way for both students and their instructor to evaluate progress. I have therefore devoted an entire part of the text (Part Seven) to a series of objective tests, and I have included a second series of these tests in this *Instructor's Manual*. These tests, starting on page 00, may be photocopied.

9   I think a strong attendance policy is vital for a developmental skills course. Following is part of an information sheet that I distribute to new classes:

> This is a skills course—not a lecture course where you can borrow a friend's notes afterward. Typically, one or more skills will be explained briefly in class, and you will then spend most of the class time practicing the skills, making them your own. You will be learning in the best possible way: through doing.
>
> Since much of the value and meaning of the course is the work done in class, you must be here on a steady basis. In a real sense, if you miss class, you are missing the course. Therefore, you should determine now to attend class faithfully; otherwise, you will be wasting your time and money.
>
> Grading will be tied in with attendance. Quizzes will be given at the start of, and during, many classes. If you are late or you miss class, you will receive a zero. Makeup tests will, as much as possible be provided upon request. However, makeup grades will never count for as much as in-class grades.

When I started teaching this course a number of years ago, I made attendance a voluntary matter. Many of my students, not able to handle the winds of freedom, were blown away. I now believe that a firm attendance policy, tied in closely to grading, is in the best interest of most students.

A MODEL SYLLABUS

Following is a syllabus I have used as a general guide for the use of *Reading and Study Skills* with my reading students at Atlantic Cape Community College. The syllabus assumes a three-hour class meeting once a week for fifteen weeks. It also assumes time for review of homework activities or matters covered in previous classes. The first nine weeks of the course emphasize study skills, for these are skills that students need immediately for help with their other classes.

Very seldom are *all* the skills listed for a single class covered in that class. Instead, I focus on those skills most suited to the needs of the individual students involved. Instructors using the book will probably want to do likewise, emphasizing the skills most appropriate for their students.

Class 1

- Business matters. I hand out 4- by 6-inch slips of paper on which students write their names, addresses, and phone numbers; other courses they are taking; whether they are working full- or part-time; and their likely career goals.

- Introduction to the instructor and the course.

- Class exercise: The memory-building activity described on page 1 of this *Instructor's Manual*.

- Skill introduced: "Taking Classroom Notes." I advise students to take notes from the very start in their other classes. To underscore the importance of notetaking, I put the relentless facts about forgetting on the board (80 percent forgotten in two weeks; 95 percent in a month—see page 43). I suggest that students have a separate notebook (or section of a looseleaf book) for each course, and I cover briefly several other organizational hints (pages 43–45).

- Skill introduced: "Time Control and Concentration." I tell students to get a large monthly calendar, or make one. (I show them my own—a Sierra Club Wilderness Calendar with plenty of write-in space.) I also pass out more 4- by 6-inch slips and give students practice in preparing a "to do" list— a helpful skill, for they have a lot of items to remember at the very start of the semester.

- Assignment: To get *Reading and Study Skills* for the course and to fill in the "Guide to Courses" on the inside back cover of the book.

Class 2

- Skill covered: "Taking Classroom Notes." I put students into groups of fours, and they read the thirteen note-taking hints (as described on pages 43 ff.). I put on the board a grid and ask someone from each group to write in the group's choices for the five most important note-taking hints. Here's the way the grid looks:

	Jack's Group	Betty's Group	Carol's Group	Maurice's Group
Most important				
Second most imp.				
Third most imp.				
Fourth most imp.				
Fifth most imp.				

The grid is then used as a basis for class discussion of the note-taking hints. There is no correct sequence, except that Hint 1 should be in the first position. The sequence depends upon the needs and priorities of individual groups of students. The value of the grid is that it gets students to think actively about all the note-taking hints, and it's a good focal point for discussing the hints.

I also cover methods for studying class notes (pages 51–54 and Activity 2 on pages 62) and handwriting efficiency (pages 52–57). Note that students are more interested in handwriting efficiency if it's presented with the sexier title *speed writing*.

- Skill covered: "Time Control and Concentration." I go through the activities on pages 75–78 and 83–84 (where I have students prioritize the items on Emily's "to do" list).

- Assignments:
  (1) Work through the "Introduction" on pages 1–8.
  (2) Complete "Time Control and Concentration" on pages 71–90, and do a weekly study schedule.

Class 3

- Test 1: I give students one of the classroom note-taking lectures on pages 63–69 *or* use a taped lecture prepared by a subject-area instructor on our faculty.

- Test 2: I give students ten to fifteen minutes to read and study pages 39–60 and prepare for a mastery test (pages 543–544) on taking class notes. It may be advisable to have students tear out the test (the test pages are perforated) and hand it in to you before they begin studying; you can then pass it back to them when they're ready to take the test.

- Skill covered: "Setting Goals for Yourself" (pages 20–27). I have students work in pairs or small groups and read through the entire chapter, answering the various questions as they proceed. Class discussion follows.

- Assignment: Read "Your Attitude: The Heart of the Matter" (pages 11–19) and write a paper responding in detail to one of the nine questions on page 19.

Note: In Class 3 and following classes, I cover briefly in class or assign as homework (or both) the various word skills in Part Two, as needed by students. I also begin to introduce, as time permits, the various reading comprehension skills in Part Four (pages 361 ff). The main emphasis, however, remains on study skills.

Class 4

- Skill covered: "Textbook Study I: The PRWR Study Method." I present in turn the various points in the chapter (pages 93–106), and students work through the various activities that help them learn those points. We also do Activity 1 on pages 106–108.

- Skill covered: "Recognizing Definitions and Examples" on pages 361–367.

- Test: I give students ten to fifteen minutes to read and study pages 71–90 and prepare for a mastery test (pages 545–546) on time control and concentration.

- Assignments:
  (1) Complete the activities in "Textbook Study I: The PRWR Study Method" on pages 108–112.
  (2) Do the review test on definitions and examples on pages 366–367.

Class 5

- Skill covered: "Textbook Study II: Using PRWR." We do pages 113–121 in class.

- Skill covered: "Recognizing Enumerations" on pages 368–377.

- Test: The mastery test on definitions and examples on pages 573–574.

- Assignment: Do pages 121–128 and the review test on enumerations on pages 375–377.

Class 6

- Skill covered: "Building a Powerful Memory." I demonstrate the first memory step, organization, by having students group the nine shopping items on page 210. (I write the items on the board in random order before showing students the grouped items in the book.)

- We then read and work through the rest of the chapter and do several of the activities at the end.

- Test: I give students two mastery tests in PRWR: pages 547–549.

- Assignment: We begin "Applying PRWR to a Textbook Chapter," starting on page 150, in class, and students are then asked to work through Section Three (up to page 183) for homework.

Class 7

- Skill covered: We complete the textbook chapter in class (through page 204).

- Test: I allow students to use their notes to take the quiz on the textbook chapter on pages 205–206.

- Test: I give students ten to fifteen minutes to read and study pages 207–218 in preparation for a mastery test (pages 553–554) on memory building.

- Skill covered: "Recognizing Headings and Subheadings" on pages 378–390.

- Assignment: Read "Learning Survival Strategies" on pages 28–35 and write a paper responding in detail to one of the last five questions on page 36.

Class 8

- Skill covered: "Taking Objective Exams." I always challenge students when they do Activity 1 on page 230. I explain that no student has ever followed all ten of the directions questions correctly, but that if anyone does, I will on the spot give him or her an A for the course, and he or she may leave the classroom and not come back for the rest of the semester. So far, at least, no one has ever gotten all ten correct, but everyone has energetically tried.

- Test 1: I give students two tests on taking objective exams—the mastery tests on pages 555–556 and 559–560. I count only the grade of the one on pages 559–560.

- Test 2: I also test students on headings and subheadings, using the review test on pages 388–390 and the mastery test on pages 577–578. Again, I count only the second grade.

- Skill covered: "Recognizing Signal Words" (pages 391–400).

- Assignment: Do the review test on signal words on pages 399–400.

Class 9

- Skill covered: "Taking Essay Exams." I teach this unit by having students prepare their own outline of hints on taking classroom notes (taken from the thirteen hints on pages 43–51).

- Test: Students then study for and write an essay answer to the question, "Write an essay describing seven hints to remember when taking classroom notes." We then compare their answers with the answer on page 252.

- Assignments: Do Activity 4 on taking essay exams on page 254.

Class 10

- Skill covered: "Using the Library and the Internet." I lecture on the library and Internet for about half an hour, and we then descend *en masse* on the library and do most of the activities there. Students realize that they should ask questions about anything they don't understand, for they're preparing themselves to do the individualized (and graded) research activity that follows.

- Assignment: Each student chooses a different area to research from the activity on pages 274–276.

Class 11

- Test 1: Students have half an hour to prepare an outline answer for the question on page 557 and to study the outline. They then write an essay answer to the question.

- Test 2: Students are given ten to fifteen minutes to read and study pages 255–274 in preparation for a mastery test (pages 561–562) on the library and the Internet.

- Skill covered: "Recognizing Main Ideas" (pages 401–408).

- Assignment: Do the review test on main ideas on pages 407–408.

Class 12

- Test: Mastery test on main ideas on pages 581–582.

- Skill covered: "Knowing How to Outline." We go through pages 409–419.

- Skill covered: "Knowing How to Summarize." We go through pages 424–435.

- Assignments:
  (1) Do the review test on outlining on pages 420–423.
  (2) Do the review test on summarizing on pages 436–438.

Class 13

- Test 1: Mastery test on outlining on pages 583–584.

- Test 2: Mastery test on summarizing on pages 585–588.

- Skill covered: "Skim Reading." The five timed passages on pages 457–473 are extremely helpful in making students apply the comprehension skills learned in Part Four. If they do not take advantage of definitions, enumerations, and relationships between headings and subheadings, they will not take effective notes.

- Assignments:
  (1) Individualized work in the college reading lab. Any make-up work.
  (2) As needed, "Understanding Graphs and Tables" on pages 439–451 or any of the additional learning skills in Part Eight of the book.

Class 14

- Skill covered: "Rapid Reading." We do the first four selections on pages 485–502.

- Test: Skim-reading mastery test on pages 591–592.

- Assignments:
  (1) Individualized work in the college reading lab. Any make-up work.
  (2) As needed, any of the additional learning skills in Part Eight of the book.

Class 15

- Skill covered: "Rapid Reading." We do two additional selections chosen from those on pages 503–534.

- Test 1: Rapid-reading mastery test on pages 593–596.

- Test 2: Department-required final reading exam.

ANSWER KEY

PART ONE: MOTIVATIONAL SKILLS

Setting Goals for Yourself

p. 22   (Activity)

      1. Vocational preference test—points to careers that match your interests and abilities.
   2–5. Answers will vary.

p. 23   (Activity 1)

     1. Study and/or personal
     2. Study
     3. Study
     4. Study
     5. Personal
     6. Study
     7. Study and/or personal
     8. Study and/or personal

pp. 24–27 (Activities 2–5)

    Answers will vary.

PART TWO: STUDY SKILLS

Taking Classroom Notes

p. 43   Getting down a written record of each class is essential because **forgetting begins almost immediately.**

p. 44   Sitting near the front **helps you stay tuned to what the instructor does in class** and also **encourages you to take notes.**

p. 45   Reading the textbook in advance of a lecture **helps you to understand challenging material and to take more organized and effective notes.**

p. 46   Answers will vary.

p. 47   Indentation means **setting in from the margin secondary points and supporting details.**

pp. 48–50 Answers will vary.

p. 51   It is important to go over your notes soon after class because **they are still clear in your mind; you can then make them more complete and better organized.**

pp. 51–52   What is an important assumption of economics?
            What are two types of economic resources?

p. 55   S = Skinner; beh = behaviorism

p. 62   (Activity 2)

      5 sources of truth
      Def. and ex. of intuition
      Def. of authority
      2 kinds of authority and defs.
      2 kinds of secular authority and defs.

pp. 63–64   (Activity 4)

1. People lose attention.
2. Talking—125 wpm; listening—500 wpm.
3. Summarize. Try to guess what's next. Question the truth of what's been said.
4. Make a conscious effort to listen closely.

pp. 65–66   (Activity 5)

1. Messages intended to persuade audiences to adopt a certain opinion
2. Testimonial, bandwagon, plain folks, and transfer
3. People are encouraged to do or buy something because "everyone else is doing it."
4. Products are associated with something attractive, respectable, or admired.

pp. 67–68   (Activity 6)

1. a. Make a point.
   b. Support your point.
   c. Organize your supporting details.
   d. Write clear, correct sentences.
2. "Be specific."
3. Time order and emphatic order
4. Saving the best or most important detail for last

Time Control and Concentration

p. 76   A monthly calendar will keep you constantly aware of exam and paper target days, so that you can **prepare** (*or* **plan**) **for them well in advance**.

p. 76   (Activity)

Answers will vary, but Emily could gain three hours of study time by using some of the time slots below:
9:00–10:00 a.m.   11:00 a.m.–1:00 p.m.   7:30–11:30 p.m.

p. 79   15 class hours
            23 study hours

p. 80   14 separate blocks
3 different benefits

Sunday (7:00–10:00 p.m.)

Monday (4:00–5:00 p.m.); Tuesday (9:00–10:00 a.m.); Wednesday (10:00 p.m.–bedtime); Thursday (3:00–4:00 p.m.); Sunday (10:00 p.m.–bedtime)

The question about Emily's rewarding herself with a free day is a matter of individual choice. Many people feel it is a good idea to have a full day's break in a busy weekly schedule. On the other hand, keep in mind that if you are so busy on occasion that you need Saturday study time to keep up with your work, you should not hesitate to take the time.

p. 81   In any one of the three study blocks that Emily has on Thursday
Morning study hours
Saturday evening
Sunday morning or later Sunday evening

p. 84   Answers will vary, but items 1, 2, 3, 4, 6, and 13 should be labeled *A*.

Textbook Study I: The PRWR Study Method

p. 99   (Activity 2)

1. The selection is about **alternatives to conflict**.
2. a. accommodation
    b. assimilation
    c. amalgamation
3. a. displacement
    b. toleration

p. 101   (Activity 1)

1. You should mark off definitions, examples, and enumerations because **these are among the most important ideas in a selection**.
2. You should not underline examples because **you need to distinguish them from definitions**.

p. 103   (Activity 1)

1. Write down **every** heading in the chapter.
2. Enumerations are items in a list.
3. Answers will vary.
4. Answers will vary.

p. 104   (Activity 2)

Missing notes:
1a. Ex.—threat of war to end internal conflicts and bring national unity
2. Assimilation—two-way process by which people and groups come to share a common culture.
3. Amalgamation—biological interbreeding of two groups until they become one

p. 106 (Activity)

1. Answers will vary.
2. Answers will vary.
3. Go back and make sure you can still recite the first four definitions.
4. Recall words are **key words and phrases that help you remember what is in your notes**.
5. Write recall words **in the margins of your notes**.

p. 106   (Activity 1: A Short Passage from a Speech Text)

Fill-ins: types of noise; four

Noise—any stimulus that gets in the way of sharing meaning
1. External noises—stimuli that draw people's attention away from intended meaning
   Ex.—sound of airplane overhead
2. Internal noises—thoughts and feelings that interfere with meaning
   Ex.—daydream
3. Semantic noises—alternative meanings aroused by certain symbols that inhibit meaning
   Ex.—"gay fellow" interpreted as "homosexual"

Def of noise; def + ex of external noise, internal noise, semantic noise

See if you can say to yourself the definition of *noise*.

p. 108   (Activity 2: A Short Passage from a Sociology Text)

Fill-ins: the crowd; four

Crowd—a temporary, relatively unorganized gathering of people who are close together
1. Casual crowd—participating in a common event
2. Conventional crowd—assembled for a specific purpose and acting according to established norms
3. Expressive crowd—gotten together for self-stimulation and personal gratification
4. Acting crowd—engaged in rioting, looting, or other forms of aggressive behavior

types of crowd behavior

p. 109   (Activity 3: A Short Passage from a Psychology Text)

Fill-ins: types of ESP; four

1. Telepathy—one person's sending thoughts to another
   Ex.—looking at picture and trying to "send" it to someone in another room
2. Clairvoyance—perceiving distant events
   Ex.—sensing one's child has been in a car accident
3. Precognition—preknowing future events
   Ex.—predicting the assassination of a political leader
4. Psychokinesis—"mind over matter"
   Ex.—levitating a table

def and ex of ESP; 4 types of ESP

See if you can say to yourself the definition and an example of *telepathy*.

p. 110   (Activity 4: A Short Passage from a Social Psychology Text)

    Fill-ins: seeing ourselves favorably; *self-serving bias*

    Self-serving bias—the tendency to perceive oneself favorably

        Ex.—Scrabble player thinks he wins because of verbal skill, but thinks he loses because the game has a high element of chance.

    example

p. 111   (Activity 5: A Short Passage from a Business Text)

    Fill-ins: factors of production; four

    Factors of production—a society's resources

1. Land—real estate, minerals, timber, and water
2. Labor—human resources used to produce goods and services
3. Capital—machines, tools, and buildings used to produce goods and services, as well as money that buys other resources
4. Entrepreneurs—the ones who develop new ways to use the other resources more efficiently

    factors of production

Textbook Study II: Using PRWR

p. 114   *Catchword:* CELL (Answers may vary.)

p. 115   *Catchphrase:* **T**ed's **c**at **p**urrs **p**owerfully. (Answers will vary.)

p. 117   (Activity for Reading 1)

    Preview: the stages of the business cycle; none; one; three
    Write: The notes required are apparent in the text itself.
    Recite: Sample catchphrase: Pick red roses.

p. 119   (Activity for Reading 2)

    Preview: anger; three; three
    Write: The notes required are apparent in the text itself.
    Recite: Sample sentence: Whenever I approach the cat, she most commonly avoids me.

p. 121   (Activity for Reading 3)

    Preview: norms; one; six
    Write: The notes required are apparent in the text itself.
    Recite: Sample catchphrase: Fred is my friend.

p. 123   (Activity for Reading 4)

    Preview: illnesses; four; three (pancreatitis, cirrhosis of the liver, alcoholic hepatitis)
    Write: The notes required are apparent in the text itself.
    Recite: Sample sentence: Mice greatly love garbage.

p. 125 (Activity for Reading 5)

Preview: matter; two; five; *nucleus*
Write: The notes required are apparent in the text itself.
Recite: Key words: def. and ex. of elements; def. and ex. of atoms; 3 types of
subatomic particles; def. of nucleus.

p. 142 (Quiz on Reading 1)
    1. c   2. d   3. False   4. b

p. 142 (Quiz on Reading 2)
    1. a   2. b   3. c   4. a

p. 143 (Quiz on Reading 3)
    1. d   2. False   3. False   4. c

p. 144 (Quiz on Reading 4)
    1. c   2. False   3. d   4. c

p. 144 (Quiz on Reading 5)
    1. True   2. a   3. c   4. d

p. 145 (Quiz on Reading 6)
    1. a   2. d   3. b   4. True

p. 145 (Quiz on Reading 7)
    1. c   2. b   3. a   4. d

p. 146 (Quiz on Reading 8)
    1. b   2. False   3. b   4. False

p. 147 (Quiz on Reading 9)
    1. c   2. c   3. b   4. False

p. 147 (Quiz on Reading 10)
    1. b   2. a   3. d   4. d

Textbook Study III: Applying PRWR to a Textbook Chapter

p. 150
- Number of major heads: six
- Subheads under DIVORCE: four
- First boldface italicized term: **family**
- First italicized term in Section 1: *regulation of sexual activity*
- Number of tables, figures, and photographs: 23
- Number of boxes with related material: 3
- Introduction: yes
- Summary: yes
- List of key terms: yes

p. 158   (Activities for Section 1)

Fill-ins: 155, 157

(Chapter 11: The Family)

CROSS-CULTURAL SIMILARITIES AND DIFFERENCES

The form the family takes and the functions it performs vary widely over time and among societies.

     Ex.—One tribe in East Africa considers it normal for a man to ask permission to sleep with a good friend's wife. *(Other examples are also possible.)*

Family Structure
1. *Monogamy*— marriage involving only one woman and one man
2. *Polygamy*— marriage involving more than one wife or husband at the same time
   Kinds of polygamy:
   a. *Polygyny*—marriage of one man to two or more women
       Ex— up to 1890, the Mormons of Utah
   b. *Polyandry*— marriage of one women to two or more men
   c. *Group marriage*— marriage of two or more men to two or more women at the same time—the rarest family type
3. *Serial monogamy*—one exclusive, legally sanctioned, but relatively short-lived marriage after another

Family Functions in Traditional, Preindustrial Societies:
1. Regulation of sexual activity
2. Reproduction
3. Socialization of children
4. Providing for the physical needs of both young and old members

Changes in Traditional Family Functions in Modern, Industrial Societies:
1. Birth control and abortion now make regulation of sexual activity less urgent.
2. Sex before marriage now considered permissible by most Americans.
3. Schools and day care centers now provide socialization and preparation for occupations; mass media also a factor.
4. Government and medical establishment have taken over some of former economic functions of family, such as care for sick and elderly.

A function that has become important in modern society—emotional gratification

p. 160   (Comments on Section 1)

      examples
      75%

p. 172   (Activities for Section 2)

Fill-ins: 157, 171

THE AMERICAN FAMILY IN HISTORICAL PERSPECTIVE

The Extended Family—members of three or more generations, related by blood or marriage, who live together or near one another
The Modified Extended Family —networks of relatives that establish separate residences but maintain ties
The Nuclear Family—a husband, wife, and their dependent children living in a home of their own

Contemporary Families:
3. *Single-parent families—have nearly doubled in the last* 20 *years*

Ethnic and Racial Variations:
3. *Asian American families:*—patriarchal; men earn money, make decisions, and discipline children; women do housework and child-rearing; children taught to be cooperative and obedient; high rate of marriage; low rate of divorce

p. 174   (Comments on Section 2)

      twelve *pages* . . . boldface *type*
      166 . . . 167 . . . 167 . . . 170
      single *people*

p. 182   (Activities for Section 3)

Fill-ins: 171, 181

COURTSHIP, MARRIAGE, AND CHILDREN

Choosing a Mate
In most societies, marriages are arranged.

Why do we marry? Because of the principle of homogamy—the tendency to marry someone who is like ourselves in the social attributes our society considers important.

Work and Families
2. *Child care:* In 1995, 21 million American children under age 6 had mothers working outside the home. Result: more children cared for by relatives or day care.
3. *The impact of work on families:*
    The most important care for infants and toddlers is either a single caregiver or a small group.

p. 189   (Activities for Section 4)

Fill-ins: 181, 188

BEHIND CLOSED DOORS: VIOLENCE IN THE FAMILY

Myths and Realities

2. *Myth 2:* Abusers are mentally ill.
   Fact: Only about 20 percent of abusers are clinically diagnosed as mentally ill.

3. *Myth 3:* Abuse occurs only in poor, minority families.
   Fact: Abuse occurs in families at all socioeconomic levels.

4. *Myth 4:* The real causes of family violence are alcohol and drugs.
   Fact: Only one illegal drug has been linked with increased aggression; alcohol does not itself cause abuse but is often used as an excuse for violence.

   (Note: The authors of the text lose their focus a bit here; they should more clearly make the point that alcohol is not the cause as such for much family violence.)

5. *Myth 5:* Children who are abused grow up to be abusers.
   Fact: They are more likely to be abusive, but this does not mean that all violent adults were abused as children, or that all abused children grow up to be violent.

6. *Myth 6:* Battered women provoke their offenders, and/or the solution is for them to leave their partners..
   Fact: It is not easy for a battered wife to simply walk out the door; we've been slow to build shelters for them.

Sociological Explanations
Five factors contribute to violence in the family:

1. *Intimacy*—Family members are intensely involved with one another; when quarrels break out, the stakes are higher than in other social groups.

2. Privacy—Because family affairs are regarded as private, there are few outside restraints on violence and often few people around to observe and try to stop abuse.

3. Inequality—Within a family, men are usually stronger than women and women are stronger than children; they can get away with violence that persons of equal strength would resist.

4. Social and cultural support for the use of physical force in the family. A marriage license in our society is a license to hit—not just children, but spouses.

5. Socialization—we learn to associate violence with the family; our first experience of force nearly always takes place at home.

Intimate Violence: The Victims
Infants and young children *are at greatest risk of abuse.*

p. 200   (Activities for Sections 5 and 6)

Fill-ins: 188, 199

DIVORCE

Understanding Divorce Statistics
Divorce rate—The number of divorces per 1,000 married women (or men) in a given year.
> *Ex.*—In 1994, the rate was 20.5 divorces per 1,000 married women.

Main factors affecting likelihood of divorce:
1. Age at first marriage—couples who married in teens much more likely to divorce than couples in their twenties.
2. Socioeconomic status—divorce rates are highest in the lower socioeconomic groups.
3. Race—African American couples (more likely to be young and poor when they marry) are more likely to separate or divorce than white couples.
4. Religion—in general, the more often a person attends religious services, the less likely he or she is to divorce.
5. Children—couples without children have the highest divorce rate.

p. 204   (Closing Comments)

To do so, put key *(or* recall) *words in the margin.*

Your purpose would be to study until you could recite *to yourself the family structures and family functions without looking at them.*

After completing each page of notes, you should go back and review *the previous pages.*

p. 205   (Quiz on the Sample Chapter)

1. False	6. b. arranged by older relatives
2. b. polygyny	7. b. like ourselves in important ways
3. b. a husband, a wife, and their children	8. False
4. False	9. c. socioeconomic status
5. c. both of the above	10. c. intimacy and companionship

Building a Powerful Memory

p. 211   Material in your class notes and textbooks should be **organized** in some meaningful way before you attempt to memorize it.

p. 212   You would go back and test yourself on the ones you had memorized so far.

p. 216   Catchwords for the techniques in behavior therapy (**e**xtinction, **i**mitation, **r**einforcement, and **d**esensitization) might be DIRE or RIDE. (Answers may vary.)

p. 216   A catchphrase for the influences on a child (**p**arents, **s**iblings, **f**riends, **r**elatives, **t**eachers) might be **P**aul **s**anded **F**ran's **r**ough **t**able. (Answers will vary.)

18

p. 217   Step 5: You might study for two hours; then, review the material within a day for an hour or two; finally, review several days later for the remaining two or three hours.

p. 218   Step 6: ten
Step 7: Most students might find it more realistic to use the technique just in the review periods before exams.

p. 218   (Activity 1)

1. One catchword for the goals of punishment (**r**etribution, **d**eterrence, **i**ncapacitation, and **r**ehabilitation) might be DIRR.
2. One catchword for the characteristics of schizophrenia (**l**anguage-thought disturbances, **d**elusions, **p**erceptual disorders, **e**motional disturbances, and **i**solation) might be PILED.
3. A catchphrase for the six avoidance tactics (**c**an't, **b**usy, **t**ired, **l**ater, **b**ored, **h**ere) might be **C**arol **b**ought **t**wo **l**ovely **b**aby **h**amsters.

p. 219   (Activity 2)

1. A catchphrase for the theory of human needs (**b**iological, **s**afety, **c**ompanionship, **e**steem, **a**ctualization) might be **B**ob's **S**iamese **c**at **e**ats **a**nchovies.
2. A catchphrase for the six stressful experiences (**d**eath of spouse, **d**ivorce, **m**arital separation, **j**ail term, **d**eath of close family member, **p**ersonal injury or illness) might be **D**on't **d**rive **m**y **J**eep **d**owntown, **P**aul.
3. A catchphrase for the seven steps in research (**d**efine, **r**eview, **f**ormulate, **p**lan, **c**ollect, **a**nalyze, and **d**raw) might be **D**riving **R**ay's **F**ord, **P**ete **c**lipped **a** **D**atsun.

p. 220   (Activity 3)

1. Catchwords for the five factors about the audience (**l**arge, **i**nterest, **k**nowledge, **a**ttitude, and **p**erceive) might be PALIK or LIKAP. A catchphrase might be **L**arry **K**ing **p**repares **a**ll **i**nterviews.
2. A catchword for the four personal zones (**i**ntimate, **p**ersonal, **s**ocial, **p**ublic) might be SIPP. A catchphrase might be **I** **p**refer **S**panish **p**eople.

p. 222   (Activity 4)

A catchword for the four stages in getting a job (make **c**ontact, **w**ritten materials, **i**nterview, **t**hank-you note) might be CWIT.
A catchword for the four ways to make contact (**p**lacement bureau, want **a**ds, telephone **c**alls, and personal **c**onnections) might be PACT.
A catchphrase for the two types of written materials (**r**ésumé, **c**over letter) might be **R**obbers **c**reep.
A catchword for three interview guidelines (**e**tiquette, **r**esponses to questions, come across as a **c**ompetent person) might be REC.
A catchword for the four typical interview questions (**w**hy are you interested, what are your greatest **s**trengths and weaknesses, tell me about **y**ourself, why should we **h**ire you) might be YISH.

Taking Objective Exams

p. 227   You are unlikely to forget material during exams if you are **well prepared**.

p. 230   (Activity 1)

> *A Note to the Instructor:*
>
> I always challenge students when they do the short activity on p. 230. I explain that no student has ever gotten all ten of the "following directions" questions correct, but that if anyone does, I will on the spot give him/her an *A* for the course, and he/she may leave the classroom and not come back for the rest of the semester.

1-2.   _____   _____Langan, John_____
                        Langan, John
                         (written)   (printed)

3.   twelve (written out, not in figures)
4.   (A lot of people fold the page, and only afterwards see instruction 6. They have not "First read all the instructions carefully.")
5.   Survivors are not buried.
7. $5
8.   One birthday a year (like everyone else)
9.   seven (or 7). Many people include the second sentence as well as the first.
10.   The moral of this question is: If you don't understand a question, ask the instructor to clarify it. The correct response for this question is for the student to raise his/her hand and say, "What does number 10 mean?" or "I don't understand number 10."

p. 240   (Activity 2)

1.	False	*Hint:*	F
2.	c	*Hint:*	A and C
3.	a or b	*Hint:*	D
4.	True	*Hint:*	E
5.	c	*Hint:*	A and C
6.	b	*Hint:*	E and F
7.	d	*Hint:*	A
8.	True	*Hint:*	E
9.	a	*Hint:*	A
10.	False	*Hint:*	F

Taking Essay Exams

p. 246   important

p. 247   (Activity)

supporting material . . . word . . . letter . . . tested . . . idea

p. 248   (Activity)

1.   b.   Give a series of points and number them 1, 2, 3. . .
2.   d.   Show differences between two things.
3.   e.   Give the formal meaning of a term.
4.   c.   State briefly the important points.
5.   a.   Tell in detail about something.

p. 251   (Activity)

1.   is about
2.   corrections . . . dictionary
3.   First, Also, Second, Next, A fourth hint, Another hint, A sixth hint, Finally

p. 254   (Activity 2)

There are seven hints to remember when taking classroom notes. *(Always begin with a sentence that tells what your paragraph is about—a topic sentence.)* First of all *(use word signals to introduce each hint)*, you should be in class on a regular basis. Reading a friend's notes cannot substitute for the experience of having ideas presented and explained to you in class. This is the most important single step to taking good notes and doing well in a course. *(Add supporting details to help explain the value of each hint.)* A second hint is to read your text in advance. The text gives you a good initial sense of a topic to be presented in class. You will understand more of what a teacher is saying and will probably be able to take more effective notes. A third hint is to write down the teacher's examples. They should be marked with an *Ex.* The value of the examples is they help you to understand abstract points. Another hint, a basic one, is to get down in general a written record of the class. This is crucial because in two weeks we forget up to 80% of what we hear. *(Note that the uncorrected essay gives supporting details for this hint but not the hint itself.)* A fifth hint is to review notes soon after class. The reason is to make your notes as clear as possible while they are still fresh in your mind. Check to make sure that the organization is clear and that all connecting information needed to understand the notes is present. A sixth hint is to write down the connections between ideas. If you don't, you are almost sure to forget them, and you will have trouble understanding your notes later on. Always write down connections the teacher may make at the start or close of a class. Label these "Preview" or "Review," as the case may be. Finally, do not stop taking notes at the end of a class. Teachers may use this time to cover important points they wanted to present in class but did not because of time spent in class discussion.

Note: Comments that explain some of the corrections made in the student essays have been enclosed within parentheses and italicized in the rewritten essay above.

Using the Library and the Internet

p. 260   (Activity)

Part A. 1.   Answers will vary.
2.   By author, by title, or by subject
3.   By subject

Part B. 1.   Answers will vary. One example: *Our Character, Our Future: Reclaiming America's Moral Destiny.*

2.   Answers will vary. One example: *How the Garcia Girls Lost Their Accents.*

3.   John Irving

4.   Judith Guest

5.   Answers will vary. Two examples: *Acid Rain,* Sally Morgan; *The Late, Great Lakes: An Environmental History,* William Ashworth.

6.   Answers will vary. Two examples: *Fidel: A Critical Portrait,* Tad Szulc; *The Untold Story of Fidel Castro,* Georgie Anne Geyer.

7.   Answers will vary, but the following are possibilities:

Adopted	*Style*	*Generation*
a. Jill Krementz	William Strunk and E.B. White	Tom Brokaw
b. Knopf	Macmillan	Random House
c. 1982	1999 (4/e); earlier eds. 1959, 1972, 1979	1998
d. 362.7 KRE	808 STR	940.548 B
e. Adoption	English language—Rhetoric	World War II

8.   Answers will vary, but the following are possibilities:

Schlessinger	*Trillin*	*Hawking*
a. *How Could You Do That?*	*Family Man*	*A Brief History of Time*
b. HarperCollins	Farrar Straus Giroux	Bantam
c. 1996	1998	1988
d. 170.44 S	814 T	523.1 H
e. Character; Courage, Conscience	Child rearing, Family life	Cosmology

p. 262   (Activity)

	1.	2.	3.	4.
Library of Congress System:	1. c	2. b	3. a	4. a
Dewey Decimal System:	1. b	2. c	3. a	4. d

p. 265   (Activity 1)

1.   Find books on your topic.
2.   Find articles on your topic.

Answers to all other activities in this chapter will vary.

PART THREE: A BRIEF GUIDE TO IMPORTANT WORD SKILLS

Understanding Word Parts

pp. 296–300   (Prefixes)

1 mono / 2 trans
a. translated
b. monopolize
c. transported
d. monopoly
e. transcend

3 dis / 4 pre
a. discards
b. predict
c. discomposed
d. prejudge
e. disinfect

5 inter / 6 sub
a. interval
b. subdue
c. interrupting
d. subheads
e. interfere

7 ex / 8 mis
a. misconduct
b. misrepresented
c. execute
d. mistreated
e. exterminator

9 con / 10 post
a. postmortem
b. conglomeration
c. postoperative
d. conform
e. conspiring

11 anti / 12 pro
a. proposal
b. antifreeze
c. procreation
d. promote
e. antidote

13 un / 14 ad
a. adhesive
b. uncertainty
c. addiction
d. unrestrained
e. unproductive

15 in / 16 extra
a. extraordinary
b. extracurricular
c. inadequate
d. ingratitude
e. informal

17 re / 18 mal
a. malnutrition
b. recovery
c. malfeasance
d. review
e. reinforcement

19 com / 20 de
a. Communal
b. demolished
c. demeaned
d. comply
e. depreciated

Note: Answers to the second part of each set will vary.

pp. 301–306 (Suffixes)

1 ion / 2 less

   a. tension
   b. penniless
   c. persuasion
   d. careless
   e. motionless

3 ant / 4 ness

   a. sadness
   b. reluctant
   c. deodorant
   d. suddenness
   e. Abundant

5 en / 6 ize

   a. memorize
   b. soften
   c. strengthen
   d. darken
   e. immortalize

7 age / 8 ist

   a. marriage
   b. Communist
   c. specialist
   d. leakage
   e. columnist

9 ment / 10 ful

   a. government
   b. forgetful
   c. excitement
   d. grateful
   e. improvement

11 ship / 12 able

   a. workmanship
   b. comfortable
   c. friendship
   d. recyclable
   e. hardship

13 ence / 14 ify

   a. excellence
   b. reference
   c. clarify
   d. justify
   e. dependence

15 ate / 16 ly

   a. cultivate
   b. quickly
   c. perpetuate
   d. finally
   e. generate

17 ious / 18 or

   a. counselor
   b. mysterious
   c. obvious
   d. inventor
   e. actor

19 ism / 20 ery

   a. tomfoolery
   b. terrorism
   c. alcoholism
   d. cemetery
   e. plagiarism

Note: Answers to the second part of each set will vary.

pp. 306–311 (Roots)

1 duc / 2 mit
- a. introduction
- b. conductor
- c. remit
- d. transmitted
- e. committee

3 port / 4 voc
- a. vocation
- b. advocate
- c. portable
- d. Reporters
- e. supporting

5 tract / 6 auto
- a. attract
- b. distractions
- c. autobiographies
- d. detracts
- e. autonomous

7 path / 8 cept
- a. sympathy
- b. apathetic
- c. except
- d. reception
- e. accepted

9 dict / 10 script
- a. description
- b. predictions
- c. manuscript
- d. contradict
- e. inscription

11 vers / 12 tang
- a. tangled
- b. versatile
- c. tangible
- d. reversal
- e. diversion

13 cess / 14 sist
- a. persistence
- b. assistant
- c. recess
- d. procession, successfully
- e. resistant

15 gress / 16 pend
- a. aggressive
- b. pendant
- c. digressions
- d. impending
- e. dependent

17 psych / 18 vid
- a. evident
- b. psychosis
- c. video
- d. psychic
- e. psychosomatic

19 spec / 20 graph
- a. retrospect
- b. inspector
- c. respect
- d. polygraph
- e. paragraph

Note: Answers to the second part of each set will vary.

p. 312 (Activity 1)

transparent

disorient

exclamation

compatible

deceptive

antiseptic

preliminary

malpractice

confusion

reversal

replacement

subdivision

extrasensory

conductive

interpretation

Using the Dictionary

p. 314 (Spelling)

guidance	accomplish
writing	accept
aggressive	environment
pleasant	particular
accommodate	conscious
program	article
disease	necessary
beginning	challenge

p. 314 (Syllabication)

spar-kle	(2 syllables)
hyp-no-tize	(3 syllables)
ex-or-ci-sm	(4 syllables)
op-por-tu-nis-tic	(5 syllables)

p. 315 (Vowel Sounds)

(Common words will vary depending upon the dictionary used. The ones below are taken from *The American Heritage Dictionary*.)

pet	toe
tie	cut
pot	boot

p. 316 (The Schwa)

Answers will vary for words containing schwa sounds.

p. 316 (Accent Marks)

kə nōt′	rĭ sĭp′rə kəl
ăd mŏn′ĭsh	ĕk străv′ə găn′zə
bĭ hē′məth	pŏl′ē ŭn săch′ə rā′tĭd

p. 316 (Full Pronunciation)

tickle	question
worry	exit
dessert	keyboard
meatball	fictitious
	luxury

1. kō′jənt	6. loo′krə tĭv
2. fē ăs′kō	7. něm′ə sĭs
3. răsh′ə năl′	8. dĕp′rĭ kāt
4. ăt′rə fē	9. lĕth′ər jē
5. trĕn′shənt	10. rə pā′shəs

Note: Alternative pronunciations are possible for some words.

26

p. 317 (Parts of Speech)

noun
plural
singular

p. 318 (Principal Parts of Irregular Verbs)

begin	began	begun	beginning
steal	stole	stolen	stealing
eat	ate	eaten	eating

p. 318 (Plural Forms of Irregular Nouns)

apologies
wives
hypotheses
formulas *or* formulae
passers-by

p. 318 (Meanings)

1. containing many small bubbles of gas
2. sparkling, high-spirited
3. preliminary action
4. short composition serving as an introduction

p. 319 (Etymology)

sandwich—from the First Earl of Sandwich, who had "sandwiches" of bread and beef brought to him so he would not have to leave the gambling tables for meals.

breakfast—from the Middle English word *brekefast*, meaning "to break one's fast," usually by eating in the morning.

p. 320 (Usage Labels)

rough—Informal
finagle—Informal
hang-up—Informal
ain't—Nonstandard
cool—Slang

p. 320 (Activity 1)

1. ĕn kō′mē əm
2. kô′stĭk
3. kən jĕk′shər
4. pər nĭsh′əs
5. rōk′fərt
6. vər bā′tĭm
7. ə môr′fəs
8. prī mē′vəl
9. măk′ ĭ nā′shən
10. dĭs′ ĭn jĕn′yoō əs

27

p. 320   (Activity 2)

1. four
2. on the third syllable (zĭsh)
3. on the last syllable (zā)
4. pat
5. d. toe
6. d. long *e.*
7. a. long *a.*
8. False
9. True
10. explicit
11. a. Meaning 1
12. b. Meaning 2
13. b. Noun meaning 2
14. c. Meaning 3

Word Pronunciation

p. 324   (Background Information)

nos-tril (2 syllables)
Fran-ken-stein (3 syllables)
con-tem-po-ra-ry (5 syllables)

p. 325   (Activity: Divide between Double Consonants)

1. cen / ter
2. pol / len
3. hor / rid
4. twit / ter
5. pres / sure
6. um / ber
7. ac / rid
8. ger / mane
9. sten / cil
10. tur / bid
11. fer / vent
12. spec / tral
13. grem / lin
14. vis / cous
15. trans / ves / tite

p. 325   (Activity: Divide before a Single Consonant)

1. co / gent
2. e / voke
3. hu / mid
4. le / thal
5. sa / vor
6. su / ture
7. i / rate
8. so / lace
9. pa / thos
10. fru / gal
11. de / claim
12. mi / mo / sa
13. lu / mi / nous
14. ma / tron
15. cre / ma / tion

p. 326   (Review Test)

1. ad / vo / cate
2. de / sist
3. con / do / lence
4. fes / ti / val
5. non / par / ti / san
6. si / ne / cure
7. rep / ri / mand
8. pa / tel / la
9. in / con / clu / sive
10. las / si / tude
11. cur / so / ry
12. scru / ti / nize
13. co / los / to / my
14. in / con / tro / ver / ti / ble
15. phe / no / bar / bi / tal

p. 326   (Rule 3)

straight / for / ward
whole / sale
ev / er / green
mon / key / shine
strong / hold
news / print

p. 326   (Rule 4)

head / ing
spine / less
state / ment

ex / hume
dis / con / tent
re / vers / able

syn / drome
sub / merge
an / ti / bi / ot / ics

p. 326   (Rule 5)

ne / on
ob / vi / ous

co / op / er / ate
ve / ne / re / al

duo / de / num
ac / tu / ar / y

p. 327   (Activity 1)

1. de / ter' / gent
2. vo / ra' / cious
3. bul' / wark
4. prog / nos' / ti / cate
5. ful' / some
6. fur' / tive
7. vi / cis' / si / tude
8. con' / sum / mate
9. fab' / ri / cate
10. ca / jole'
11. nu' / ance
12. sa' / li / ent
13. em / bel' / lish

14. in / ad / ver' / tent
15. re / pu' / di / ate
16. post / pran' / di / al
17. a / lac' / ri / ty
18. a / bor' / tive
19. pug / na' / cious
20. pro' / mul / gate
21. cas' / ti / gate
22. oc / to / ge / nar' / i / an
23. ab / ste' / mi / ous
24. scur' / ri / lous
25. as' / pi / rant

p. 328   (Activity 2)

Terms from Psychology

1. en / gram
2. sen / so / ry
3. ger / mi / nal
4. pre / na / tal
5. a / ver / sive

6. sib / ling
7. li / bi / do
8. vis / ce / ral
9. ol / fac / to / ry
10. sub / li / ma / tion

Terms from Sociology

1. mar / gi / nal
2. dis / sent / er
3. ac / com / mo / da / tion
4. kib / butz
5. a / mal / ga / ma / tion

6. de / mog / ra / phy
7. hal / lu / ci / no / gen
8. ge / sell / schaft
9. hos / pice
10. com / part / men / ta / li / za / tion

Terms from Biology and Other Sciences

1. cor / tex
2. mi / to / sis
3. ru / bel / la
4. pep / tide
5. his / ta / mine

6. in / su / lin
7. es / tro / gen
8. der / ma / ti / tis
9. he / ma / to / ma
10. pla / cen / ta

1. sur / tax
2. fis / cal
3. mer / can / tile
4. con / ver / gence
5. in / den / ture
6. con / sump / tion
7. mer / ger
8. ag / gre / gate
9. Mal / thu / si / an
10. de / cen / tra / li / za / tion

Spelling Improvement

p. 335 (Activity: *I* before *E*)

1. friend
2. ceiling
3. brief
4. mischief
5. retrieve
6. relieve
7. receive
8. thief
9. achieve
10. hygiene

p. 336 (Activity: *Final E*)

1. describing
2. loner
3. caring
4. immensely
5. likeness
6. arrival
7. usable
8. peaceful
9. servicing
10. retirement

p. 336 *Fill-in:* consonant . . . y . . . i

p. 337 (Activity: *Y* to *I*)

1. flies
2. hurried
3. emptiness
4. easier
5. tried
6. worries
7. readiness
8. babies
9. prettier
10. beautiful

p. 338 (Activity: Doubling)

1. bigger
2. shopped
3. swimming
4. compelled
5. beginning
6. forgetful
7. equipped
8. repellent
9. committed
10. shipment

p. 338 (Final Activity)

1. regretting (Rule 4—Doubling)
2. sipped (Rule 4—Doubling)
3. deceit (Rule 1—*I* before *E*)
4. studies (Rule 3—*Y* to *I*)
5. merely (Rule 2—Final *E*)
6. relied (Rule 3—*Y* to *I*)
7. robbery (Rule 4—Doubling)
8. receipt (Rule 1—*I* before *E*)
9. forgotten (Rule 4—Doubling)
10. nervous (Rule 2—Final *E*)

Vocabulary Development

p. 341   good vocabulary.

p. 342   contexts. (Answers to the remaining items will vary.)

p. 345   the context in which the word appears.

pp. 346 (Activity 1)

1. c. Unknowing (The misinterpretation about elbow grease is not a matter of carelessness; it is simply a matter of not knowing.)
2. d. Thrifty
3. c. Pretended
4. a. Huge
5. c. Nonsense
6. d. Friendly
7. b. One who likes pain
8. d. Indifference
9. d. Inclined to revenge
10. a. Recent (The context clue here is the second part of the sentence: "I should have cited some *up-to-date* research on my topic.")

p. 348 (Activity 2)

1. conflicting
2. equal or surpass
3. harmless substances given to humor a patient
4. disrespectful; belittling
5. repetitive; wordy

p. 348 (Activity 3)

1. d. Return
2. a. Incorrectness (The word *overlooks* is a context clue that helps you understand that *fallacy* means "incorrectness.")
3. d. Respectful
4. b. Discourages
5. a. Medical forecast
6. c. Prosperous
7. b. Unconquerable
8. a. Distributing (The context clues here include *ration*, *distribute*, and *divide them equally*.)
9. a. Increase
10. a. Set in a belief

p. 351   vocabularies.
             defined . . . glossary . . . index
             your course notebook.

p. 354   Answers will vary.

PART FOUR: READING COMPREHENSION SKILLS

Introduction

p. 359   Good comprehension seldom happens all at once but is usually a **process**.
There are eight skills you can learn to improve your **understanding of what you read**.

p. 360   1. Comprehension is something that should happen all at once.
2. An increase in reading rate means an automatic increase in reading comprehension.

With difficult material, understanding is likely to fall as the rate rises.
Develop reading comprehension skills.

Skill 1: Recognizing Definitions and Examples

p. 362   You should **underline** definitions.
Examples help clarify abstract definitions.
An example that makes sense and "works" for you.

p. 362   (Activity 1)

1. Territoriality refers to persons' assumptions that they have exclusive rights to certain geographical areas, even if these areas are not theirs by legal right.
    Ex.—Students consider certain seats to be "their" territory.
Personal space refers . . . to the space surrounding our body, a space that moves with us.
    Ex.—Persons sitting in a public reading room try to have at least one empty seat between themselves and the next reader.

2. The allness fallacy is the attitude that what we know or say about someone or something is all there is to know and say.
    Ex.—Smug sophomore who thinks he has studied all about botany.

3. Potential energy is stored-up energy or energy an object possesses due to its relative position.
    Ex.—Water backed up behind a dam
Kinetic energy is energy that matter possesses due to its motion.
    Ex.—Moving water can drive generators.

4. Positive transfer—what a person has learned to do in one situation applies equally well in another situation.
    Ex.—Jokes that work in introductory psych class also work in personality psych class.
Negative transfer—what works in one situation is not applicable to another situation.
    Ex.—Jokes fall flat at faculty club.

Note: One example is shown for most selections. Additional examples are sometimes possible.

p. 364   (Activity 2)

    1. The effort to completely exterminate a people by killing all of them is called annihilation.
        Ex.—Nazis tried to annihilate Jews.

    2. Vacillation—the tendency to be drawn first toward one possible resolution of the conflict, then toward another.
        Ex.—Trying to decide whether to work or to go out with friends.

    3. Token economy—hospitalized psychiatric patients receive rewards for performing "normal" behaviors.
        Ex.—Patient receives tokens for working in hospital laundry and can trade them for weekend passes, etc.

    4. A wave is a periodic disturbance—a back and forth change of some kind—that spreads out from a source and carries energy as it goes.
        Ex.—Water waves moved outward from a stone splashing into a lake.
        (Other examples: Sound waves carry the noise of a clap; light waves light up a room.)

p. 365   (Activity 3)

Answers will vary.

p. 366   (Review Test)

1	Definition:	2	Example:	3
2	Definition:	11	Example:	1
3	Definition:	1	Example:	2
4	Definition:	5	Example:	2

Skill 2: Recognizing Enumerations

p. 369   They are often keys to important ideas.

They tell you that an enumeration is coming (and help you write the heading that describes what the list is about).

p. 370   (Activity 1)

    1. Heading: Types of Income
      1. Money income
      2. Real income
      3. Psychic income

    2. Heading: Elements in Networking
      1. Visibility
      2. Familiarity
      3. Image

    3. Heading: Forms of Water Pollution
      1. Garbage and chemicals
      2. Thermal (warm-water)

4. Heading: Reasons for the Existence of Stereotypes
    1. Simplify explanations of human behavior
    2. Provide a scapegoat for aggressions
    3. Give members of a dominant group a sense of superiority

p. 372 (Activity 2)

1. Functions of Private Property in Capitalism
    1. Places in the hands of individuals power over the use of productive resources
    2. Serves an an incentive for the accumulation of wealth

2. Negative Results of Physical Punishment
    1. May lead to anger and frustration
    2. May lead to aggressive acts against "safe," nonpunishing objects
    3. May extend only to behavior in presence of parents

3. Responses to Criticism
    1. Withdraw
    2. Justify yourself
    3. Counterattack

4. Steps in Solving a Complex Problem
    1. Identify the problem.
    2. Search for possible solutions.
    3. Analyze the situation.
    4. Move to the attack itself.

p. 375 (Activity 3)

Answers will vary.

p. 375 (Review Test)

1. Approaches to Treating the Allergic Patient
    1. Control the environment.
    2. Use drug therapy or chemotherapy.
    3. "Desensitize" the patient.

2. Why Children of Divorce Often Live Disrupted Lives
    1. Must deal with trauma of parents' separation
    2. Have only one parent to turn to on daily basis
    3. Must deal with continuing conflict between parents

3. Stages of Human Development
    1. Embryonic—first two months after conception
    2. Fetal—third month to birth
    3. Neonatal—first four weeks after birth
    4. Infancy—first two or three years of life

4. Forms of Patterned Violence Within the Tribe
    1. Chest-pounding duel—take turns hitting each other with fists (legal violence)
    2. Club fights—take turns hitting each other with clubs (regulated warfare)
    3. Raid—actual warfare, with aim of killing one individual from another village

Skill 3: Recognizing Headings and Subheadings

p. 379   (Activity)

1. 2 main heads; 9 subheads. (10 subheads if a student counts the "Questions to Consider.")
Main heads are set in larger type than subheads.

2. 3 subheads
3 subsubheads
Subsubheads are italicized.

3. Answers will vary.

p. 381   Doing so is a way of getting at the main idea (cutting through a mass of words to the heart of the matter).

The relationship between a main head and subheads may express a main idea in a selection.

"Focus Your Listening": three subsubheads; suggestions for how to focus your listening.

"Convenience Products": three subsubheads; types of convenience products.

p. 382   (Activity 1)

1. In writing, any idea that you advance must be supported with specific reasons or details.

2. Learning the student accomplishes for himself, for his own ends with little or no regard for extrinsic reasons for learning

Example: Boy who knows fifty football plays by heart and yet cannot conjugate a verb

3. Job boredom can be overcome through job enlargement and job enrichment.

4. More than 65 percent of the labor force

Profit-oriented and marketing-oriented businesses

p. 384   (Activity 2)

Note: Some likely questions are presented below. Other questions are, of course, possible.

Sociology

1. a. What is a primary group?
   b. What is a secondary group?
   c. How do the two relate to each other?

2. a. What are some prison abuses?
   b. What is the reform movement?
   c. When was the reform movement started?

3. a. What is social knowledge?
   b. What are the barriers to social knowledge?
   c. Which is the most important barrier to social knowledge?

4. a. What are the beneficial impacts of cities?
   b. What are the negative impacts of cities?
   c. What kind of impact is greater?

Psychology

5. a. What causes loneliness in modern life?
   b. Who is affected by this loneliness?
   c. What are the results of this loneliness?

6. a. Who are the social dropouts?
   b. Why do they become dropouts?
   c. What are some ways of preventing people from dropping out?

7. a. What are some ways of coping with frustration?
   b. What are the effects of not coping?
   c. What kind of person does the best job of coping?

8. a. What is mental retardation?
   b. What are the causes of mental retardation?
   c. What can be done about mental retardation?

History and Political Science

9. a. What were the Dark Ages?
   b. What was the glimmer of light in the Dark Ages?

10. a. Why was Roosevelt elected to a second term?
    b. What were the achievements of Roosevelt's two terms?
    c. What were the failures of Roosevelt's two terms?

11. a. What is the Fourteenth Amendment?
    b. When was it passed?

12. a. What caused the War of 1812?
    b. How long did the war last?
    c. What countries were involved?

Business and Economics

13. a. What are the types of economic systems?
    b. Is one preferable to the others?

14. a. How does business contribute to pollution?
    b. How can pollution by business be regulated?
    c. How serious and widespread is pollution by business?

15. a. What is the Taft-Hartley Act?
    b. When was it passed?
    c. What were its values and drawbacks?

16. a. How is business regulated?
    b. Should business be regulated?

17. a. What are the characteristics of living things?
    b. What is the most basic characteristic of living things?

18. a. What causes cell development?
    b. What interferes with cell development?
    c. In what ways does a cell develop?

19. a. What is energy?
    b. Are there different kinds of energy?

20. a. What is heart disease?
    b. What causes heart disease?
    c. How can heart disease be prevented or controlled?

p. 385   (Activity 3)

Answers will vary.

p. 386   (Activity 4)

Note: The order of the lettered sections may vary.

A. Urban Problems
   1. Pollution
   2. Strikes
   3. Crowding
   4. Slums

B. Conquest of the Plains
   1. The Sheepherders
   2. The Cattle Kingdom
   3. Frontier Farmers
   4. Prospectors and Ranchers

C. Noncommunicable Diseases
   1. Heart and Artery Disease
   2. Arthritis
   3. Cancer
   4. Diabetes

D. Techniques in the Writing Process
   1. Preparing a Scratch Outline
   2. Brainstorming
   3. Making a List
   4. Freewriting

E. Kinds of Body Units
   1. Cells
   2. Tissues
   3. Organs
   4. Organ Systems

p. 387 (Activity 5)

Answers will vary.

p. 388 (Review Test)

A.   *Wording of answers may vary.*

1. An estimated 1.3 million teenagers and preteens drink to excess. Problem drinkers among teenagers are more often found among students who also engage in other types of deviant behavior, value and expect achievement less and value independence more than nondrinkers, and who are more tolerant of deviant behavior in others; girls who are problem drinkers are likely to have parent problems.

2. The myth of acceptance states that the worth of one's actions is judged by the approval they bring. It's a myth because it isn't true, and acting on it causes one to lose the affection and respect he or she wants.

B.   *Note*: Some likely questions are given below. Others are, of course, possible.

Our Changing Life Span
a. What is our life span today?
b. What factors are causing it to change?

Children of Divorce
a. How many children of divorce are there?
b. In what ways does divorce affect children?

Corporate Cover-Ups
a. Which corporations have been involved in cover-ups?
b. How have corporations tried to hide their behavior?

Industrial Revolution
a. When did the Industrial Revolution take place?
b. What were the effects of the Industrial Revolution?

C.

A. Advertising Media
   1. Television
   2. Direct Mail
   3. Magazines

B. Problems of Adolescence
   1. Dropping Out of School
   2. Drug Abuse
   3. Juvenile Delinquency

C. Altered States of Consciousness
   1. Sleep
   2. Meditation
   3. Hypnosis

Skill 4: Recognizing Signal Words

p. 392 (Activity: Emphasis Words)

1. one of the most important assumptions
2. especially in terms of health
3. the most crucial
4. most widespread

p. 393 (Activity: Addition Words)

1. First . . . Moreover . . . Furthermore
2. First of all . . . Also . . . Another . . . In addition . . . Finally

p. 394 (Activity: Comparison or Contrast Words)

1. in a similar fashion . . . In contrast
2. Just as . . . But
3. In like manner . . . On the other hand
4. just as . . . Still

p. 395 (Activity: Illustration Words)

1. For example
2. for instance
3. such as
4. To illustrate

p. 396 (Activity: Cause-and-Effect Words)

1. because
2. as a result
3. Thus
4. If . . . then

p. 397 (Activity 1)

Emphasis	*Addition*	*Comparison*
most important	moreover	alike
most significant	also	just as
especially valuable	in addition	similarly

Contrast	*Illustration*	*Cause and Effect*
but	for example	therefore
differ	for instance	as a result
however	such as	consequently

p. 398 (Activity 2)

1. Consequently (cause and effect)
   on the other hand (contrast)

2. most persistent (emphasis)
   For instance (illustration)
   But (contrast)
   Also (addition)

3. The greatest value (emphasis)
   However (contrast)
   As a result (cause and effect)

4. reasons, Consequently (cause and effect)
   First, Second, Third, fourth (addition)
   However (contrast)

p. 399 (Review Test)

1 1. however
   2. In addition
   3. most vital
   4. for instance
   5. Yet

2 1. Consequently
   2. important
   3. However
   4. For example

3 1. Because
   2. important
   3. One
   4. Another
   5. Finally
   6. For example

4. 1. Yet
   2. First
   3. Second
   4. Still
   5. As a result
   6. But

40

Skill 5: Recognizing Main Ideas in Paragraphs and Short Selections

p. 403   1. a main idea
          2. reasons or details that develop the idea

The main idea most often appears in the **first** sentence of a paragraph.

p. 404   (Activity 1)

1. During the Depression, money shortages produced important changes in the daily lives of people.

2. Fear seems to break down normal rational behavior.

3. In our society a person who wishes to marry cannot completely disregard the customary patterns of courtship.

4. But even on a simple level, being honest is not always easy.

Note: The first sentence provides the definition of *integrity*, but it is not the main idea of the selection. If it were the main idea, the selection would consist of a number of examples of integrity. In fact, the material in the selection is devoted to showing how "being honest is not always easy."

p. 405   (Activity 2)

1. d. Little scientific evidence exists to support a belief in ESP.
2. d. To a great degree, TV has affected the structure and makeup of daily life.
3. d. The mentally ill have been mistreated through history.
4. b. Some scientists believe that hostility is biological, but many believe that it is learned.

p. 407   (Activity 3)

Answers will vary.

p. 407   (Review Test)

1. 1 Little in American society remained untouched by World War II.

2. 2 But many children with disabilities still are not receiving the education that could help them to become fully functioning members of society.

3. 5 It seems pretty clear that smoking is harmful not only to the smoker but also to the fetus.

4. 6 Regardless of how well you listen, you can be overloaded with details.

Skill 6: Knowing How to Outline

p. 412 (Activity)

1. To make them visually clear, so you can see them "at a glance."
2. consistently indented under
3. title.

p. 414 (Activity 1)

1. Social and Economic Classes in the South
   1. Aristocracy of large planters
   2. Lesser planters, professionals, business and industrial leaders
   3. Middle and lower-middle class: yeoman farmers, skilled mechanics, and tradespeople
   4. Poor whites and free blacks
   5. Slaves

2. *Special Costs in Buying a House*
   1. Title search
   2. Closing costs
      a. Lawyers' fees
      b. Real estate agent's commission
      c. Taxes paid in advance
      d. Expenses of filing records
   3. Property insurance
      a. Flood
      b. Fire
      c. Burglary
      d. Protection against lawsuits
   4. Special assessments at settlement
      a. Sewers
      b. Sidewalks
      c. Community parks

3. *Getting Psychological Help*
   1. Ask for recommendations
      a. Instructor
      b. School counseling service
      c. Physicians
      d. Clergy
   2. Check out reputations
   3. Call the professionals
      a. Ask about training, degree, experience
      b. Ask about approaches and goals
   4. Exploratory visit

p. 417   (Activity 2)

1   EASY WAYS TO LOSE WEIGHT

Eliminate milk and sugar from coffee.
Use nonstick pots and pans.
Avoid high-calorie salad dressings.
Substitute broiling or baking for frying.

2

Normal   Neurotic

KINDS OF DEPRESSION

Psychotic

Bipolar depressive disease   Unipolar depressive disease

3   DANGER SIGNS OF ALCOHOLISM

Initial Phase   Crucial Phase   Chronic Phase
  Increasing consumption
  Morning drinking
  Regretted behavior
  Blackouts

p. 420   (Review Test)

1   Subcultures of High School Students
  1. Fun subculture
  2. Academic subculture
  3. Delinquent subculture

2   Costs of Being Nonassertive

  1. Social costs
  2. Psychological costs
     a. Withdrawal
     b. Becoming cynical
     c. Despair
  3. Physiological costs
     a. Psychosomatic illnesses
     b. Stress-related diseases

3   SMOG

Smoke and fog   Photochemical smog
                          Carbon monoxide
                          Nitrogen dioxide
                          Ozone

4   SIGNS OF AGING

Bone structure stiffens.

Skin and muscles lose elasticity.

Fat accumulates.

Sensory defects occur.
Vision changes.
Hearing loss occurs.

Skill 7: Knowing How to Summarize

p. 425   A summary **reduces** a large quantity of material to the most important points. Unless you fully **understand** the material you are reading, you will not be able to summarize it.

p. 425   (Activity 1)

    A. 1. b. Who Are the Poor?
        2. c
    B. 3. a. Our Vanishing Water Supply
        4. b
    C. 5. c. Trichinosis and Its Prevention
        6. a
    D. 7. b. The Priming Method of Memory
        8. b

p. 428   (Activity 2) *Wording of answers may vary.*

    A. *Heading:* Active Listening
      Summary: Active listening is hard work, for it requires the listener to concentrate on, think about, and sometimes repeat what is being said.
    B. *Heading:* Social Norms
      Summary: Patterns of social behavior are controlled by social norms—shared rules or guidelines which prescribe the behavior that is appropriate in a given situation.
    C. *Heading:* The Slaughter of the Buffalo
      Summary: In the nineteenth century, vast herds of American buffalo were reduced to a mere handful by the white man's wanton slaughter.
    D. *Heading:* British Approach to Heroin Addiction
      Summary: The British treat heroin addicts very differently from Americans, putting them in the hands of medical authorities rather than law enforcement officials.

p. 430   (Activity 3)

    1. a   7. b
    2. c   8. c
    3. a   9. a
    4. a   10. c
    5. b   11. a
    6. c

p. 432   (Activity 4)

Wording of answer will vary; here is one possible summary of the article.

Due to the increased number of working parents, over two million children come home from school every day to an empty house. Responsible for taking care of themselves, these "latchkey kids" often face certain emotional problems. They may feel particularly vulnerable, having no guardian nearby to help them in emergencies or frightening situations. Moreover, as they are usually instructed to stay indoors until their parents come home, they miss out on the play and social interaction crucial in any child's development. Thus, they become bored and feel isolated. Some experts contend that these feelings of alienation may eventually lead kids to academic failure, violence, and drug and alcohol abuse. Fortunately, many parents have found ways to protect their children from the unpleasant effects of "latchkeyism." Parents can combat their children's boredom and loneliness by assigning them chores and enrolling them in after-school social programs such as scouting or dance lessons. Staying in touch by phone, identifying a neighbor to turn to in emergencies, and clearly defined rules make kids feel safer.

p. 435   (Activities 5, 6, and 7)

Answers will vary.

p. 436   (Review Test) *Wording of answers 6 and 8 may vary.*

A. 1. c. Rituals of Sacrifice
    2. b
    3. b. Education in America after the Civil War
    4. c
B. 5. c. Proximity as a Factor in Friendships
    6. *Summary:* Sheer proximity is perhaps the most decisive factor in determining who will become friends.
    7. a. Institutional Care for the Elderly: A National Disgrace
    8. *Summary:* The care given elderly people in institutions is inadequate and poorly regulated.

Skill 8: Understanding Graphs and Tables

p. 444   (Activity 1)

   1. a. The purpose of this graph is to show U.S. population growth from 1790 to 2040.
       b. 125 million
       c. 225 million
       d. 450 million
       e. 250 million

   2. a. The purpose of this table is to show how much energy appliances use per year.
       b. Least: Toaster. Most: Clock.
       c. Most: Water heater. Least: Clock.
       d. Clothes dryer
       e. Television
       f. 1000 average kW/h
       g. clock.

p. 446   (Activity 2)

   1. a. The purpose of the graph is to show the share of minorities in the U.S. population from 1900 to 2050.
       b. 12 percent
       c. 50 percent
       d. Latino
       e. Native American
       f. Asian American
       g. African American and Native American

   2. a. The purpose of the table is to show how men and women think the sexes differ.
       b. Moody
       c. 57%
       d. 54%
       e. Men: 53%; women, 37%

p. 449   (Activity 3)

   1. 28%
   2. 19% (from 6% to 25%)
   3. Largest: White (39.5%). Smallest: Native American (1.7%)
   4. From about 20 to about 44
   5. 25.9 . . 22.8 . . . 26.9
   6. 21.9 . . 20.3 . . . 24.5
   7. About 69 . . . About 39
   8. About 55 . . . About 68
   9. 250,000,000 . . . 9
  10. Paying bills
  11. 1994
  12. While the *overall* trend is a more or less steady rise, the *current* trend is **holding steady at around 22%.**

p. 450 (Review Test)

1. a. To show the distribution of household tasks by family members.
   b. 19%
   c. Wife . . . 70%
   d. Dishwashing; 26%
   e. 1%
   f. Yardwork

2. a. To compare numbers and earnings of men and women in the same occupations.
   b. 3,773,000 . . . $10,983
   c. $7,307
   d. $22,955
   e. Transportation and material moving
   f. Women: $12,250 . . . Men: $21,522

PART FIVE: SKIM READING AND COMPREHENSION

p. 456   That every word must be read.

Skimming (reading selectively for main ideas)

1. Find definitions.
2. Locate enumerations.
3. Look for relationships between headings and subheadings.
   Or: Look for points marked by emphasis words and for main ideas in what seem to be key paragraphs.

p. 457   Selection 1: "Visual Elements in Assertive Communication"

Answers to questions on page 475:

1. Any four of the following:
   Eye contact
   Distance
   Facial expression
   Gestures and posture
   Body orientation

2. Intimate distance
   Personal distance
   Social distance
   Public distance

p. 459   Selection 2: "Science and the Search for Truth"

Answers to questions on page 476:

1. Intuition
   Authority
   Tradition
   Common Sense
   Science

2. Intuition is any flash of insight (true or mistaken) whose source the receiver cannot fully identify or explain.

3. Verifiable evidence
   Ethical neutrality

4. Science may be defined as a method of study whereby a body of organized scientific knowledge is discovered.

5. A fact is a descriptive statement of reality which scientists, after careful examination and cross-checking, agree in believing to be accurate.

p. 463   Selection 3: "The Nature of Power"

Answers to questions on page 476:
1. Force
   Authority
   Influence

2. Force is physical coercion or the threat of such coercion.

3. Charismatic authority
   Traditional authority
   Legal authority

4. Influence is the ability to control the behavior of others beyond any authority to do so.

p. 466   Selection 4: "Defense Mechanisms"

Questions on Selection 4:
1. What are defense mechanisms?
2. Define suppression.
3. Which defense mechanism is the most basic one?
4. Give an example of repression.
5. List five other defense mechanisms mentioned in the selection.
6. *Fill in the blank:* Since defense mechanisms are _____, usually people are completely unaware of them.

Answers to the questions:
1. Defense mechanisms are the methods you use to protect your self-esteem.

2. Suppression is the deliberate attempt to avoid stressful thoughts.

3. Repression

4. An example of repression would be forgetting to contribute to a going-away gift for a friend you wish were not leaving; or forgetting someone's name, an appointment, a birthday or anniversary, or any event, thought, or feeling that has unpleasant associations.

5. Any five of the following would be acceptable:
   Withdrawal   Projection
   Fantasy   Displacement
   Regression   Compensation
   Rationalization   Sublimation

6. unconscious

   Note: A test on Selection 4 can be easily scored, for there are ten answers in all.

p. 425   Selection 5: "Fatigue"

Questions on Selection 5:

1. What are the three main categories of fatigue?
2. What is pathological fatigue?
3. Which category of fatigue does the tired housewife syndrome belong to?
4. What are the five areas of their lives that people can change in order to fight fatigue?

Answers to the questions:

1. Physical
   Pathological
   Psychological

2. Pathological fatigue is a warning sign or consequence of some underlying physical disorder.

3. Psychological

4. Diet
   Exercise
   Sleep
   Knowing yourself
   Taking breaks

Note: A test on Selection 5 can be easily scored, for there are ten answers in all.

PART SIX: RAPID READING AND COMPREHENSION

p. 481   **Rapid** (or **Speed**) reading is only one part of effective reading.

p. 482   Four (Answers to the second item will vary.)

p. 483   Try to read faster.

Note: Teachers timing the readings may find it helpful to put times on the board in ten- or twenty-second increments. For example, if the quickest student is going to finish a passage in about two minutes and the slowest is going to finish in about four, you might write on the board the following rows of numbers:

2:00	2:10	2:20	2:30	2:40	2:50	3:00
3:10	3:20	3:30	3:40	3:50	4:00	4:10

As students finish the selection, all they need do is look up and record the time that you are pointing to at that moment. With this technique, you do not have to call out each time and risk distracting the students who are still reading the selection.

p. 485   (Selection 1: "From the Autobiography of Malcolm X")

1. c. he didn't know enough words. (See Paragraph 2)
2. b. a miniature encyclopedia. (Paragraph 7)
3. d. All of it (Paragraph 7)
4. a. first copy them out on paper. (Paragraph 5)
5. False (Paragraph 6)
6. True (last paragraph)
7. b. read many books. (last paragraph)
8. a. became truly free even though in prison. (last paragraph)

p. 489   (Selection 2: "The Fine Art of Complaining")

1. d. Complaining succeeds if you know how to complain and whom to complain to. (See paragraph 4)
2. b. be polite but firm. (Paragraph 5)
3. a. act as if they expect their problem to be fixed. (Paragraphs 5, 6, and 8)
4. d. are persistent. (Paragraph 13)
5. True (Paragraph 10)
6. d. use a little flattery. (Paragraph 8)
7. c. are used by ordinary citizens. (Paragraph 10)
8. c. complaining takes effort. (Paragraph 4; the selection goes on to discuss letter writing, including obtaining the names of the appropriate people to write to, and small-claims court suits, both of which involve effort.)

p. 494   (Selection 3: "Learning to Keep Your Cool During Tests")

1. a. How to Overcome Test Anxiety (See paragraph 4)
2. b. Text anxiety can be controlled. (Paragraph 4)
3. c. stretch and then relax your arms and legs. (Paragraph 5)
4. b. underline the important instructions. (Paragraph 9)
5. True (Paragraph 1)
6. b. anxiety is learned behavior that can be unlearned. (Paragraph 4)
7. d. Budget your time for each part of the test. (Paragraphs 9, 10)
8. c. caffeine can increase anxiety. (Paragraph 8)

p. 498   (Selection 4: "An Electronic Fog Has Settled over America")

1. c. The Dangers of Television (See paragraphs 4–6)
2. d. By deadening thought, television has turned us into zombies.
   (Paragraphs 4–6, 9, 13, next-to-last paragraph)
3. True (Paragraph 10)
4. b. passive. (Paragraph 13)
5. b. image. (Paragraph 14)
6. True   (Paragraph 9)
7. b. the Maguires' problem could be found in most of the households in America.
   (Paragraph 10; last paragraph)
8. c. growing passivity and weakening intellectual skills. (last paragraph)

p. 503   (Selection 5: "The Scholarship Jacket")

1. c. Although Marta had earned the scholarship jacket, she almost lost it to a less
   deserving student. (See paragraphs 2, 5, 6, 27)
2. a. Marta was being raised by her grandparents because her parents were dead.
   (Paragraph 2)
3. c. working on their own farm. (Paragraph 26)
4. False (Paragraph 8)
5. b. overjoyed. (Paragraphs 31–32, 36)
6. a. time.
7. d. was more concerned about pleasing Joann's father than being fair to Marta. (Par. 6)
8. b. a real award should not have to be bought with money. (Paragraph 19)

p. 509   (Selection 6: "Dare to Think Big")

1. b. An Encouraging Talk. (See paragraphs 7–19)
2. a. In a talk to high school students, Ben Carson encouraged them to focus on long-
   term goals. (Paragraphs 7, 8, 15, 16)
3. a. had already read Ben Carson's autobiography. (Paragraph 6)
4. a. sidetracked Dr. Carson for a while during his teenage years. (Paragraph 7)
5. False (Paragraph 3)
6. False (Paragraph 17)
7. b. planning for the future can mean giving up some pleasure today. (Paragraphs 8– 13)
8. b. the cool guy in high school wasn't thinking about his future. (Paragraphs 11–14)

p. 514   (Selection 7: "Winning the Job Interview Game")

1. c. There are several things you can do to make yourself stand out in a positive way at
   job interviews. (See paragraph 2)
2. a. Your answer to the question "Tell me about yourself" can demonstrate that you
   are well-organized.
3. d. "Softball" questions give you the opportunity to describe your good points and
   how they fit the job.
4. b. not to blame anyone for the firing during your interview. (Paragraph 11)
5. a. You will not be flustered or late and you'll have time to review your application or
   résumé. (Paragraph 5)
6. b. If you are eager to be hired and will stay with the company (Paragraph 12)
7. a. Illustration
8. a. if you blame someone else for your troubles at work, interviewers may think that
   you may be a difficult employee.

p. 519   (Selection 8: "Flour Children")

1. d. A class requiring students to care for flour-sack babies makes them realize how much hard work and commitment goes into caring for a real child. (See paragraphs 1, 2, and 9.)
2. d. are given a ten-pound flour sack. (Paragraph 2)
3. a. talked together about important questions. (Paragraph 8)
4. d. refusing to put the baby on the floor. (Paragraph 6)
5. True   (Paragraph 6)
6. d. Students must get up several times each night to check on their babies. (Paragraphs 2–3)
7. c. is supported by the school administration. (Paragraph 5)
8. a. students who have taken the class have fewer teenage pregnancies than those who haven't (Paragraphs 4–5).

p. 524   (Selection 9: "From Nonreading to Reading")

1. c. The Story of a Marginal Reader (See paragraph 1)
2. d. Despite coming from an unsupportive home and having a learning disability, Abbott is learning to read.
3. b. he respects his wife's judgment when she buys books for their daughter.
4. b. One obstacle to Abbott's reading was his family's lack of support for school and the family members' use of drugs and alcohol.
5. c. can read only enough to get by. (Paragraph 1)
6. False (Paragraph 8)
7. b. Addition
8. b. may deal better with the disability once it is fully identified. (Paragraph 11)

p. 529   (Selection 10: "What You Need to Know to Succeed at Math")

1. b. Keys to Doing Well in Math. (See paragraphs 1, 4, 8, etc.)
2. d. Successful math students understand that math must be approached differently from other subjects. (Paragraphs 1, 4, 8, etc.)
3. a. Math is rarely useful in everyday life. (Paragraph 8)
4. b. expect students to take more responsibility for their own success. (Paragraphs 14, 22)
5. False (Paragraph 19)
6. c. building a house. (Paragraph 5)
7. False (Paragraphs 15–16)
8. b. many students fail in math because they approach it like other courses.

A Note to the Instructor:

I suggest that as students read the selections, you provide constant reminders that their focus should be on rate development (reading at maximum speed). Otherwise, some people will be seduced by certain high-interest selections into slowing down their reading. You may want to point out that in another reading situation, where the purpose of reading is not to increase rate, students might reasonably choose to read some of the articles slowly, so as to enjoy details or mull over ideas.

PART SEVEN: MASTERY TESTS

p. 541 (Motivational Skills)

1. b. is the most important factor in doing well in school.
2. short-term
3. True
4. b. geared toward an area with promising employment opportunities.
5. False
6. d. one course
7. True
8. mature
9. c. is sometimes the best response.
10. b. "I'm too disorganized."

p. 543 (Taking Classroom Notes)

1. write down
2. Ex
3. textbook
4. e. All of the above
5. c. be there and take effective notes.
6. True
7. b. Pick out key recall words on each page and write them in the margin.
    c. Make up brief study notes on each page of notes.
8. indenting
9. True
10. s-a or SA= self-actualization

p. 545 (Time Control and Concentration)

1. Exam dates and paper deadlines
2. b. Use a daily or weekly "To Do" list.
    d. Use a large monthly calendar.
    f. Make up a weekly study schedule.
    g. Consult course outlines.
3. False
4. b. slightly tense position.
5. c. 60 minutes.
6. d. all of the above will happen.
7. A place where you will see them every day.
8. c. decide on priorities.
9. False
10. d. your task is broken down into manageable units.

p. 547 (Textbook Study I)

1. c. Write down important ideas.
2. True
3. False
4. c. labeled *ex* in the margin.
5. underlining
6. numbers
7. False
8. read
9. write
10. words and phrases (*or* recall words)

p. 548   (Textbook Study II)

      Step 1:   statuses; three
      Step 3:   Study notes on "Statuses"
              Status—a position an individual occupies in a social structure
              Two kinds of social statuses
              1. Achieved
                  Ex.—*Any of the following:* senator, sanitation-man, concert pianist, coach, wife, divorcee, convict, junkie, high school dropout
              2. Ascribed
                  Ex.—gender, race, age
      Step 4:   Achieved status, ascribed status

p. 550   (Textbook Study III)

      Step 1:   Four subheads; five italicized terms
      Step 3:   Study notes on "Reasons for Forgetting"
              1. Repression—unconsciously motivated forgetting
              2. Suppression—a conscious effort to avoid thinking about an event
              3. Amnesia—loss of memory including forgetting personal information that would normally be recalled
              4. *Interference—Forget because other information interferes with your learning.*
                a. Proactive interference—previous memories block the recall of more recent learnings
                    Ex.—Want to call new Professor Kassel by name of your old girlfriend Flora Belle.
                b. Retroactive interference—recent learning blocks the recall of previous memories
                    Ex.—want to call Flora Belle "Professor"
      Step 4:   One catchword for the four reasons for forgetting: SARI
              One catchphrase for the two kinds of interference: **P**anthers **r**un.

p. 553   (Building a Powerful Memory)

    1. organize
    2. b. test yourself on the material to be learned.
    3. False
    4. b. going over a lesson you already know.
    5. hooks
    6. b. Intending to learn.
    7. d. do all of the above.
    8. bed
    9. RIP (*or* IRP *or* PIR)
  10. **S**ally **is** **so** **p**roper. (Many catchphrases are, of course, possible.)

p. 555   (Taking Objective Exams)

1. False (Hint: D)
2. True (Hint: C)
3. d. an expanding market combined with the presence of inefficient firms. (Hint: A)
4. b. insulin, an enzyme needed to use sugar properly. (Hint: B)
5. True (Hint: C)
6. c. found more job opportunities open and benefited from the movement for equality fostered by the war. (Hint: B)
7. False (Hint: D)
8. c. emotions, values, or expectations regarding self-control. (Hint: B)
9. False (Hint: D)
10. d. established the Reconstruction Finance Corporation to make loans to businesses. (Hint: A)

p. 557   (Taking Essay Exams)

Important Points about a Weekly Study Schedule:

1. Hour of study time for hour of class time (change later if needed)
2. Regular study time (definite study hours essential for success)
3. One-hour blocks of study time (takes while to get warmed up)
4. Reward for study (research shows rewards help—e.g., TV after study)
5. Study before and after class (preview and review)
6. Difficult subjects when most alert (do hard math if alert at 8 P.M.)
7. Balance activities (free time for friends, sports, etc. as well as work time)
8. Flexible schedule (trade, don't omit, times)

Sample Essay Answer:

There are eight points to remember when planning a weekly study schedule. First, plan one hour of study time for each hour of class time. Add or deduct more time later as needed. Secondly, have regular study time. Definite study hours are essential for success in school. Next, study in at least one-hour blocks of study time. In shorter time blocks, too much time might be spent just in getting warmed up. Another point to remember is that you should reward yourself for study. Research shows that a reward such as watching TV after work helps encourage you to study. Fifth, study before and after class. You'll get more out of a lecture if you read a textbook chapter before it, and if you review and add to your notes after the lecture. Another point is to study difficult subjects when you're most alert. For example, you should work on a hard math chapter at 8 P.M. if that's a time when you're very alert. Seventh, balance activities. Allow free time for sports, friends, and so on in your schedule as well as work time. Finally, keep your schedule flexible. Be ready to trade (but not omit) work times and free times in your schedule depending on the situation. Following the above hints will help you develop a study routine that should lead to good grades in school.

p. 559 (Taking Objective and Essay Exams)

1–2. _____Langan, John_____   _____
                (written)   Langan, John
                                                    (printed)

  3. e. Compare
  4. f. Illustrate
  5. a. Define
  6. c. Direction words
  7. d. List
  8. g. Summarize
  9. study
10. first
11. most important
12. budget (*or* plan)
13. True
14. True
15. False
16. False
17. c. concentrate on details in your class and text notes.
18. b. absolute statements are often false.
19. d. do all the above.
20. d. all the above.

p. 561 (Using the Library and the Internet)

1. b. Title search under *W* for *Walk*.
2. True
3. call number.
4. c. magazines.
5. "Who'll Care for Dad?"
6. *Newsweek*
7. pp. 56–57
8. November 6, 2000
9. d. do all of the above.
10. True

p. 563 (Writing a Research Paper)

  1. d. Economic benefits of the death penalty
  2. True
  3. d. all of the above.
  4. direct quotations
  5. a. list the source and page number of the information on the card.
  6. plagiarizing
  7. False
  8. c. the author's name and the page number.
  9. d. include only the books and articles referred to in the paper.
10. a. Quindlen, Anna. <u>A Short Guide to a Happy Life</u>. New York: Random House, 2000.

p. 565   (Understanding Word Parts)

1. <u>trans</u>ition
2. <u>dis</u>content
3. <u>inter</u>vene
4. re<u>tract</u>able
5. <u>tact</u>ile

6. <u>mis</u>guided
7. <u>post</u>script
8. <u>port</u>er
9. <u>Psychi</u>atrists
10. <u>in</u>edible

p. 566   (Using the Dictionary)

1. 3
2. emphySEma
3. emPIRicism
4. pit
5. noise

6. b. pet
7. c. schwa
8. True
9. a. Meaning 1
10. b. Verb meaning 2

p. 568   (Word Pronunciation)

A:						B:							
	1.	cul-prit	1				11.	vis-ce-ral	1	2			
	2.	ram-pant	1				12.	a-ver-sive	2	1			
	3.	har-bin-ger	1	1			13.	glu-cose	2				
	4.	mar-ti-net	1	2			14.	an-ti-gen	1	2			
	5.	sub-ter-fuge	1	1			15.	at-ro-pine	1	2			
	6.	con-jec-ture	1	1			16.	car-ci-no-ma	1	2	2		
	7.	im-por-tune	1	1			17.	cha-ris-ma	2	1			
	8.	ab-ro-gate	1	2			18.	ma-lig-nan-cy	2	1	1		
	9.	mas-ti-cate	1	2			19.	com-pen-sa-tion	1	1	2		
	10.	cog-ni-zant	1	2			20.	e-lu-ci-da-tive	2	2	2	2	

p. 570   (Spelling Improvement)

1. referred
2. livelihood
3. shriek
4. winning
5. cities
6. involvement
7. driving
8. safety
9. pitiful
10. niece

11. fantasies
12. rebellion
13. arrangement
14. luckily
15. writing
16. conceited
17. statehood
18. married
19. admittance
20. achievable

p. 571   (Vocabulary Development)

1. c. rude
2. b. indefinite
3. a. bare
4. d. persistent
5. c. apparent contradictions

6. b. inconsistently
7. d. organization
8. c. substitute
9. c. hindered
10. a. indifferent

p. 573   (Definitions and Examples)

1. Definition: 4   Example: 5
2. Definition: 2   Example: 3
3. Definition: 7   Example: 2
4. Definition: 2   Example: 3
5. Definition: 1   Example: 2

p. 575   (Enumerations)

1. Types of Credit Cards

   (1) Retail—e.g., department store card
   (2) Bank —e.g., Visa
   (3) Membership charge—e.g., American Express

2. Ways That Pollutants Damage the Breathing System

   (1) Slow down or stop the cilia
   (2) Build up mucus and narrow the tubes and air passages
   (3) Cause muscle spasms in the tubes of the lungs

3. Advantages of Franchising

   (1) Training and guidance given by franchisor
   (2) Customer appeal associated with well-known name
   (3) A proven idea
   (4) Financial assistance likely

p. 577   (Headings and Subheadings)

1   "Burnout" in the Professions—Answers to Questions
    1. Professionals who work extensively with human problems often feel unable to cope continually with distress.
    2. Distancing from clients; tension-related problems that include alcoholism.

2   Two meaningful questions:
    1. Emotional Problems in Childhood
        a. What are common emotional problems in childhood?
        b. What are the causes of these problems?
    2. Reconstruction in the South
        a. When did Reconstruction begin?
        b. How long did it take?
    3. Infectious Diseases
        a. What are the infectious diseases?
        b. Which ones are most common?
    4. Our Business System: Its Expansion and Regulation
        a. How does our business system expand?
        b. How is it regulated?

    Note: Other questions are possible.

3   A. The Muscular System
        1. Cardiac Muscle
        2. Skeletal Muscle
        3. *Smooth Muscle*
    B. Major Events of the Civil War
        1. The Siege of Petersburg
        2. The Battle of Gettysburg
        3. Sherman's March
    C. Behavior Disorders
        1. Paranoia
        2. Schizophrenia
        3. *Psychosis*

p. 579   (Signal Words)

1   1. But
     2. reason
     3. On the other hand
     4. Also

2   5. But
     6. In addition
     7. cause
     8. however
     9. best
    10. Also

p. 581   (Main Idea)

1. 1   Violence surrounds us—not only in real life but in our entertainment.
2. 2   There are many reasons why this child and other children can be unpopular.
3. 2   At times, however, the changes backfire and reduce rather than increase customers'
         satisfaction with the product in question.
4. 11   This self-sufficiency, or ability to provide for themselves, was a
         characteristic of many early American settlers.
5. 6   The price on the cologne box reflects not only the cost of the raw materials
         but a variety of additional costs.

p. 583   (Outlining)

Part 1: Ways to Deal with Stress

A. Work it off in physical activities.
B. Change your mental attitude.
    1. Learn to accept things.
    2. Take one thing at a time.
    3. Learn to take your mind off yourself.
C. Talk about stress and your troubles.
    1. Informally
       a. Family
       b. Friends
    2. Formally
       a. Psychologist
       b. Professional counselor

Part 2: Credit Cards *or* Advantages and Disadvantages of Credit Cards

Advantages		Disadvantages	
Obtain interest-free loans	Convenience	Billing mistakes	Temptation to overspend

p. 585   (Summarizing)

    A. 1. b. Shaping Behavior through Reinforcement
          2. b. Through a careful program of compliments, you can shape someone's behavior.
          3. c. Boss Tweed and Tammany Hall
          4. a. Tammany Hall, a corrupt nineteenth-century New York City political machine led by "Boss" Tweed, was defeated by the press.
          5. c. The Leboyer Method
          6. c. The Leboyer method of childbirth, designed to protect a newborn's delicate senses from the shock of standard deliveries, has positive effects.
    B. 7. c. Benefits of Forest Fires
          8. *Summary:* However, despite the advertising campaigns, forest fires are actually beneficial to forest ecologies.
          9. a. The Modern Refrigerator: Pluses and Minuses
       10. *Summary:* The modern refrigerator has both advantages and disadvantages.

p. 589   (Understanding Graphs and Tables)

    1. a. To show the ten fastest-growing occupations from 1990 to 2005 . . . 15 years.
        b. Corrections officers
        c. 75%
        d. Home health aides, systems analysts and computer scientists, personal and home care aides
        e. Medical assistants
        f. 30 percentage points

    2. a. To compare divorce rates in different countries from 1960 to 1994.
        b. The United States
        c. It decreased by 1.6 percentage points.
        d. Japan

p. 591   (Skim Reading)

What are the two objectives of the hospice program?
1. Keep patients free from pain on a continuous basis
2. Provide the dying with a homelike atmosphere in which to spend their final days

What are three ways that hospices reach their goals?
3. Outpatient basis
4. Inpatient basis
5. Combination of outpatient and inpatient services

What are three ways that hospices differ from other health care facilities?
6. Lack of scheduling and structure in hospices
7. Facility personnel concentrate solely on patients and don't become involved in side activities such as research and teaching.
8. View of pain control—Patients are given medication as often as necessary to keep pain from surfacing.

Also a correct answer: Hospice includes the patient's family in the care cycle.

p. 593   (Rapid Reading Passage)

1. False
2. c. allowed the military to move Japanese Americans.
3. a. American citizens.
4. d. $400 million.
5. a. second-generation Japanese Americans.
6. b. partially restored financial losses.
7. b. the government's action against the Japanese was unfair and unjust.
8. d. spy for Japan.
9. b. won more decorations than any other regiment.
10. c. deserve an official apology.

PART EIGHT: ADDITIONAL LEARNING SKILLS

Studying Mathematics and Science

p. 605   (Activity 2)

1. Additive inverse
2. Additive identity
3. Commutative property

4. Closure property
5. Associative property

p. 605   (Step 1: Preview)
1. immunity
2. eight

p. 607   (Step 3: Write)

Immunity—a group of mechanisms that help protect the body against specific diseases
1. *Antigens*—the parts of a pathogen that link up to human cells and cause damage
   Pathogens
   1) Viruses—antibodies lock onto their antigens and prevent them from entering cells
2. *T cells*
   3) Attack foreign cells, cells killed by viruses, and possibly cancer cells
Natural immunity
   Ex—Measles antibodies work only on measles virus
Acquired immunity
1. *Vaccines*—killed or weakened viruses that make body produce specific antibodies to attack antigens
   Ex—Babies must receive vaccinations after passive immunity starts to weaken.

p. 609   (Quiz on the Science Passage)

1. lymphocytes
2. vaccines
3. gamma globulin
4. antigens
5. c. lymphocyte.

6. True
7. b. antibodies.
8. c. both of the above.
9. c. both of the above.
10. b. passive immunity.

Reading Literature and Making Inferences

p. 619   (Activity)

1. b. Aunt Gladys's nephew.
2. c. twentieth-century America.
3. b. the narrator's admiration of Brenda.
4. a. a good swimmer.
5. True
6. a. about dating are old-fashioned.
7. b. in the suburbs.
8. c. both of the above.
9. b. has never met Brenda Patimkin.
10. b. have different tastes in foods.

Writing Effectively

p. 640   (Activity)

1. c. makes a point and provides specific support.
2. topic . . . thesis
3. d. all of the above.
4. True
5. scratch outline
6. b. content.
7. listing . . . time
8. d. all of the above.

THIRTY ADDITIONAL MASTERY TESTS

Material Included in This Section

The thirty additional mastery tests on the following pages can be easily reproduced on a photocopying machine. An answer key follows the tests, beginning on page 99 of this manual.

Note that the contents pages (pp iv-v) at the beginning of this manual list the tests that are provided.

Note to Instructors

Instructors who have used *Reading and Study Skills* in the past may remember a set of 30 ditto masters which accompanied the text. Because of the decreased use of ditto machines, this packet has been discontinued. We regret any inconvenience this may cause instructors.

MASTERY TEST: MOTIVATIONAL SKILLS

Answer the following questions.

1. The author feels that the single most important factor for success in college is _____

    _____

2. Unhappy and insecure in his first semester in college, the author escaped by
    a. playing games.
    b. spending time with his girlfriend.
    c. socializing with his roommate and friends.
    d. temporarily dropping out of school.

3. What are two tactics that people use to avoid doing the hard work that college requires?
    a. _____
    b. _____

4. The author says that if you are having trouble making yourself do college work, you should
    a. change your major.
    b. talk to someone about it.
    c. get a tutor.
    d. consider dropping out of school for a year.

5. When do you need to get organized during a semester?
    a. On the first day
    b. During the first few weeks
    c. When your instructor announces a test date
    d. After you receive a grade on a test

6. Specific goals consist of both personal goals and _____ goals.

7. You can find help in determining your career goals if you visit
    a. the counseling center.
    b. a faculty member in the department you have chosen as your major.
    c. the college placement office.
    d. all of the above.

8. Jean Coleman states that her friend Neil's greatest accomplishment was
    a. owning his own business.
    b. finishing college in five years.
    c. learning how to write
    d. surviving.

9. Jean Coleman's friend Nancy
    a. is optimistic that her life will improve in the future.
    b. dropped out of school after a few failures.
    c. never prepared herself for a job.
    d. has closed herself off from growth.

10. Jean Coleman says that unless a student has prepared realistically for a job after college, the chances are that there will be _____ on the doorstep waiting to offer the student a job.

> **SCORE:** Number correct (   ) x 10 = _____ %

MASTERY TEST: TAKING CLASSROOM NOTES

Some of the questions that follow are true-false or multiple-choice questions, and some require you to write short answers.

1. Of the methods listed below, which is the best way to do well in a course?
   a. Attend class regularly.
   b. Attend class and take good notes on the textbook.
   c. Attend class regularly and take good notes in class.
   d. Study the text and use someone else's class notes.

2. *True or false?* _____ It is better to wait until after a lecture to read textbook material.

3. If you do not take notes, how much of a lecture will you be likely to remember after four weeks?
   a. 80%   c. 25%
   b. 50%   d. 5% or less

4. How would you abbreviate the term *deferred gratification* during a fast-moving lecture?

   _____

5. An enumeration is
   a. anything written on the board.
   b. a list of items that fit under a particular heading.
   c. a set of notes on one unit of a course.
   d. a particular point the instructor has emphasized.

6. When you are writing notes in outline form, which of the following should start at the margin?
   a. definitions   d. definitions and main points
   b. examples   e. main points and examples
   c. main points   f. all of the above

7. *True or false?* _____ You should listen to the examples an instructor gives to illustrate ideas, but you need not write these examples in your notes.

8. An instructor may signal that a point is important by
   a. writing it on the board.   c. slowing down or becoming louder.
   b. repeating it.   d. all of the above.

9. If you miss something while you are taking notes, you should
   a. leave a blank space for it.
   b. try to think of it later that day.
   c. rely on your other notes for passing the test.
   d. forget about it and keep taking notes.

10. Which of the following is *not* described in the selection as a way to increase handwriting speed?
    a. Practice rapid writing.   c. Learn stenography.
    b. Use abbreviations.   d. Streamline your handwriting.

SCORE: Number correct ( ) x 10 = _____ %

MASTERY TEST: TIME CONTROL AND CONCENTRATION

Some of the questions that follow are true-false or multiple-choice questions, and some require you to write short answers.

1. A large monthly calendar
    a. allows you to schedule regular study periods.
    b. should be carried with you at all times.
    c. is used for exam, paper, and project due dates.
    d. is used for daily assignments.

2. A weekly study schedule
    a. should contain at least one hour of study time for each hour of class time.
    b. establishes definite study hours.
    c. includes blocks of time for relaxation.
    d. all of the above.

3. *True or false?* _____ You should keep track of your lapses of concentration during your study sessions.

4. Before you make up your weekly study schedule, you should
    a. record a typical school day to see how you are actually spending your time.
    b. see when your major projects are due and plan around them.
    c. wait to see whether you really need it.
    d. all of the above.

5. *True or false?* _____ Study sessions of ten to fifteen minutes are more effective than one-hour time blocks.

6. After a period of effective study, you should _____.

7. Study periods should ideally be scheduled
    a. only before classes.   c. both before and after classes.
    b. only after classes.   d. only in the evenings.

8. *True or false?* _____ Weekends should be set aside for recreation rather than study.

9. Your study place should
    a. be one where you can be completely relaxed.
    b. have a light source over your head or shoulder.
    c. contain a radio or tape recorder.
    d. be in a different room every day.

10. A "to do" list
    a. should be carried with you at all times.
    b. should be prepared the night before.
    c. should include priorities.
    d. all of the above.

SCORE: Number correct (   ) x 10 = _____ %

MASTERY TEST: THE PRWR STUDY METHOD

Some of the questions that follow are true-false or multiple-choice questions, and some require you to write short answers.

1. PRWR stands for (1) Preview, (2) Read, (3) Write, and (4) _____.

2. *True or false?* _____ In many college courses, the textbook is only a secondary source of information for the ideas you need to know on exams.

3. Previewing includes all the following *except*
   a. studying the title.
   b. looking briefly at words set off in *italic* and **boldface**.
   c. carefully reading charts and boxed material.
   d. reading the first and last several paragraphs.

4. *True or false?* _____ In your first reading of a chapter, you should stop at any place where you "snag" and reread until you understand that section thoroughly.

5. The purpose of marking a textbook is to
   a. set off material that you can take study notes on later.
   b. show your instructor that you have read the assignment.
   c. find the relationships between main points and examples.
   d. make sure all the material is learned, including every detail.

6. The abbreviation *Ex* in the margin means
   a. exception.
   b. excellent.
   c. example.
   d. extreme.

7. Enumerations should be marked by
   a. underlining.
   b. a vertical line in the margin.
   c. highlighting in color.
   d. 1, 2, 3, and so on.

8. *True or false?* _____ When you take study notes, you reduce a large amount of information down to the most important points.

9. When taking study notes, write down all of the following *except*
   a. definitions.
   b. examples.
   c. enumerations.
   d. secondary details.

10. To learn your notes, recite the material to yourself by using key words and phrases, which are also known as _____ words.

> **SCORE:** Number correct (   ) x 10 = _____ %

MASTERY TEST: USING PRWR

Answer the following questions by filling in the blanks.

1. A *catchword* is a word made up of the first _____ of several words you want to remember.

2. Write a four-letter catchword that would help you remember the four means of socialization: (1) family; (2) peer group; (3) educational institutions; and (4) mass media. _____

3. A *catchphrase* is a series of words, each beginning with the first _____ of a word you want to remember.

4. Write a three-word catchphrase that would help you remember in sequence the three steps in remembering: (1) encoding; (2) storage; and (3) retrieval.

_____

5-7. Read and mark the passage below. Number items in a list and write *Ex* in front of examples. Then add the three missing items in the study notes.

Adulthood

The social theorist Erik Erickson divided adulthood into three stages. In his view the central task of the first stage, young adulthood, is achieving *intimacy*. A young person who has a firm sense of identity is eager and able to fuse his or her identity with another person's in a loving relationship, without fear of competition or loss of self. A young person who avoids commitment may experience isolation. In middle age, personal and social concerns merge. Adults who feel they have contributed something of value to society and who are involved in guiding the next generation (as parents or in other roles) experience *generativity*. Those who do not experience *stagnation*—the sense of going nowhere, doing nothing important. Generativity lays the foundation for *integrity* in old age, a sense of a life well lived. Older people who have achieved integrity are satisfied with the choices they made and feel that had they a second life to live, they would "do it all over again." They see death as the final stop in a meaningful journey. For others, old age brings despair. Dissatisfied with themselves and their lives, they yearn for a second chance.

Study Notes

Stages of Adulthood: (1)_____

(2)_____

(3)_____

8. Write a catchphrase that will help you remember in sequence the three stages:

_____

SCORE: Number correct (____) x 12.5 = _____ %

MASTERY TEST: TAKING TEXTBOOK STUDY NOTES

Read the following passage. Then complete the study notes that follow it.

Unemployment

People typically find unemployment a painful experience. It may result from inability to find a first job, layoffs, dismissal because of poor job performance, or even quitting a job voluntarily. Sociologists find that unemployment has adverse effects on physical and mental health. M. Harvey Brenner has calculated that a rise of one percentage point in the national rate of unemployment, when sustained over a number of years, is associated with a 4.1 percent increase in suicide and a 4.3 percent increase in first-time male admissions to state mental institutions.

Many people pass through several stages in reacting to their unemployment. At first they undergo a sequence of shock, relief, and relaxation. In many cases they had anticipated that they were about to lose their jobs, so when the dismissal comes, they may feel a sense of relief that at last the suspense is over. On the whole they remain confident and hopeful that they will find a new job when they are ready. During this time, they maintain normal relationships with their family and friends. The first stage lasts for about a month or two. The second stage centers on a concerted effort to find a new job. If workers have been upset or angry about losing their jobs, the feeling tends to evaporate as they marshal their resources and concentrate on finding a new job. This stage may last for up to four months. But if another job is not found during this time, people move into the third stage, which lasts about six weeks. Their self-esteem begins to crumble, and they experience high levels of self-doubt and anxiety.

The fourth stage finds unemployed workers drifting into a state of resignation and withdrawal. They become exceedingly discouraged and convinced that they are not going to find work. They either stop looking for work or search for it only halfheartedly and intermittently. Then either of two responses may occur. Some people come through the stage and look back on it as a "cleansing" experience. They may make a conscious decision to change careers—perhaps by returning to school— or to settle for some other line of work. And they may look for other sources of self-esteem, including family, friends, and hobbies.

However, other people who undergo long-term unemployment often find that their family life deteriorates. Unemployment benefits end, and most Americans lose their health insurance when they lose their jobs. Financial pressures mount. People are unable to keep up their mortgage payments, or they fall behind in the rent. They see cars and furniture repossessed. It is little wonder that they feel they are losing control of their lives. Child abuse, violence, quarreling, alcoholism, and other evidences of maladjustment mount. The divorce rate soars among the long-term unemployed. Many men feel emasculated when confronted by involuntary change of roles in the family, and they lash out with destructive reactions.

Study Notes

1-4. Stages in Unemployment: (1) _____

(2) _____

(3) _____

(4) _____

5. Reactions to the fourth stage:

(1) _____

(2) Serious deterioration of family life

> **SCORE:** Number correct (   ) x 20 = _____ %

MASTERY TEST: BUILDING A POWERFUL MEMORY

Some of the questions that follow are true-false or multiple-choice questions, and some require you to write short answers.

1. The first key to effective remembering is
   a. repeated self-testing.
   b. deciding to remember.
   c. organizing the material to be learned.
   d. making up catchwords and catchphrases.

2. *True or false?* _____ Memorizing and understanding work against each other.

3. One reason why students can learn their classmates' names so easily is that
   a. some of their classmates will borrow money from them.
   b. they have made a conscious decision to learn the names.
   c. names are easier to remember than numbers.
   d. most college classes are small.

4. Repeated self-testing
   a. involves reviewing all the previous items along with the new ones.
   b. should be done after organizing the material to be learned.
   c. is a form of overlearning.
   d. all of the above.

5. If you want to remember something the next morning, you should
   a. study up to an hour before bedtime.
   b. set your clock one half hour later than usual.
   c. go to sleep right after studying.
   d. play a tape recorder with the material on it during the night.

6. Material to be learned should be _____ over several study sessions.

7. A key word
   a. is a word that is repeated throughout a selection.
   b. can be found in the table of contents of the book.
   c. stands for an idea.
   d. is made up of the first letters of other words.

8. *True or false?* _____ A catchphrase is used to recall key words.

9. Make up a catchword that will help you remember the names of the five Great Lakes: Superior, Michigan, Huron, Erie, Ontario. _____

10. Make up a catchphrase that will help you remember *in sequence* the four factors of production: land, labor, capital, and technology.

_____

SCORE: Number correct (   ) x 10 = _____ %

75

MASTERY TEST: TAKING OBJECTIVE EXAMS

All the questions that follow have been taken from actual college tests. Answer the questions by using the specific hints for multiple-choice and true-false questions that are listed below. Also, in the space provided, give the letter of the hint used to determine the correct answer.

Hints for Test-Taking

A The longest multiple-choice answer is often correct.
B A multiple-choice answer in the middle, especially one with the most words, is often correct.
C Answers with qualifiers such as *generally, probably, most, almost, often, may, some,* and *sometimes* are usually correct.
D Answers with absolute words such as *all, always, everyone, everybody, never, no one, nobody, none,* and *only* are usually incorrect.

1. *True or false?* _____ All frustrations involve conflicts.   Hint: _____

2. The Pillars of Islam are (a) located in Mecca, (b) the stages of Muhammed's life, (c) the duties and obligations Muslims must fulfill faithfully during their lifetimes, (d) Islam's sacred cities.   Hint: _____

3. *True or false?* _____ Computer speeds may be evaluated in terms of million instructions per second (MIPS).   Hint: _____

4. A manifest function of the school system is to (a) provide jobs for teachers, (b) change the class system, (c) keep young people out of the job market, (d) enable all to share the knowledge and skills once confined to the few.   Hint: _____

5. *True or false?* _____ Genetic defects can never be detected in a developing fetus.   Hint: _____

6. A satisfactory level of service is determined by (a) customer satisfaction, (b) low distribution costs, (c) the best combination of inventory and transportation costs, (d) customer demand.   Hint: _____

7. *True or false?* _____ Many people refrain from buying a product when its price appears too low.   Hint: _____

8. Foods which take the longest to pass through the stomach are (a) proteins, (b) fats, (c) carbohydrates, (d) combinations of fats and proteins.   Hint: _____

SCORE: Number correct (   ) x 12.5 = _____ %

MASTERY TEST: TAKING OBJECTIVE AND ESSAY EXAMS

You have five kinds of questions to answer on this test: following directions, matching, sentence completion, true-false, and multiple-choice.

_____   _____

1-2. *Following directions.* Write your full name, last name first, below the line on the right-hand side above. Print your full name, first name last, upside-down below the line on the left-hand side.

3-4. *Matching.* Enter the appropriate letter in the space provided next to each definition.

_____ 3. Show similarities between things.

_____ 4. Describe the development or history of a subject.

a. Contrast
b. Justify
c. Compare
d. Trace

5-6. *Fill-ins.* Write the word or words needed to complete each of the following sentences.

5. When you take an essay exam, you should always start with the _____ question.

6. You should budget your _____ before you start an exam.

7-8. *True or false.* Write "True" or "False" to the left of each of the following statements.

_____ 7. You can ignore the enumerations in your notes if you are studying for an essay exam.

_____ 8. When you have to guess the answer to a multiple-choice question, remember that the answer in the middle with the most words may be the right one.

9-10. *Multiple-choice.* Circle the letter of the answer that best completes each of the following statements.

9. If for some reason you have to cram for an exam, which of the following is the best strategy?
   a. Read through your class notes.
   b. Prepare notes on the textbook.
   c. Skim the textbook.
   d. Prepare several "cram sheets" full of important ideas to study.

10. On an objective test, you should
   a. answer more difficult questions first.
   b. never guess at answers.
   c. stick with your first answer, even if you decide it might be incorrect.
   d. try to rephrase difficult questions in your own words.

> **SCORE:** Number correct ( ) x 10 = _____ %

MASTERY TEST: USING THE LIBRARY AND THE INTERNET

Some of the questions that follow are true-false or multiple-choice questions, and some require you to write short answers.

1. In order to locate a book called *A Life on the Road,* where in the book file should you look?
   a. Under *A* in the title section
   b. Under *Life* in the title section
   c. Under *Road* in the title section
   d. Under *Life* in the subject section

2. You can best find books on a research topic by checking the (*author, title, subject*)
   _____ section of the book file, whether it is a card catalog or computer file.

3. Which of the following will be found in the reference section of the library?
   a. *Encyclopedia Americana*
   b. A back copy of *Newsweek* magazine
   c. Today's newspaper
   d. All of the above

4. *True or false?* _____ The *Readers' Guide to Periodical Literature* lists magazine articles under both subject and author.

5–8. Following is an entry from the *Readers' Guide to Periodical Literature.* Answer the questions below about the entry.

   Scientific research
   Are Human Experiments Too Dangerous? S. Begley and D. Foote. il Newsweek
   138: 38–42 Ag 6, '01

5. What is the title of the article? _____

6. Who are the authors of the article? _____

7. On what pages of the magazine does the article appear? _____

8. What is the date of the issue in which the article appeared? _____

9. A good way to use the Internet to find articles on your topic is to
   a. visit an online bookstore and use its keyword search box.
   b. use a search engine such as Google.
   c. post your topic on an online bulletin board.
   d. all of the above.

10. TRUE or FALSE: _____ A problem with Internet searches is that they often come up with too much information rather than too little.

SCORE: Number correct (____) x 10 = _____ %

MASTERY TEST: WRITING A RESEARCH PAPER

Some of the questions that follow are true-false or multiple-choice questions, and some require you to write short answers.

1. *True or false?* _____ You may have to choose another topic for your paper if there are not enough books and articles available for your research.

2. A research paper should be narrow and deep rather than broad and shallow. Which of the following topics would be best suited for a research paper of about ten pages?
   a. Drug companies
   b. Dangers of over-the-counter drugs
   c. Drugs
   d. Over-the-counter drugs

3. Two common purposes of papers are (1) to make and defend a _____ and (2) to present information on a subject.

4. When writing a scratch outline for your paper, include your thesis and
   a. your notes.
   b. your sources.
   c. areas of support for the thesis.
   d. all of the above.

5. Notes for your research paper may be in the form of
   a. direct quotations.
   b. summaries.
   c. both of the above.

6. *True or false?* _____ It is best to take notes for a research paper on both sides of each card or sheet of paper.

7. The first citation for a source in a paper must be
   a. at the bottom of the page.
   b. within the text of the paper.
   c. at the end of the paper.
   d. omitted.

8. The opening page of your paper should include an introductory paragraph that (1) attracts the reader's interest, (2) states the _____ of the paper, and (3) gives the plan of development that the paper will follow.

9. *True or false?* _____ The list of "Works Cited" at the end of a paper should include the sources you have used, arranged alphabetically.

10. Which of the following shows the correct format for a "Works Cited" entry?
    a. Kozol, Jonathan. Savage Inequalities. New York: Crown Publishers, 1991.
    b. Jonathan Kozol. Savage Inequalities. New York: Crown Publishers, 1991.
    c. Savage Inequalities. Jonathan Kozol. New York: Crown Publishers, 1991.

SCORE: Number correct ( ) x 10 = _____ %

79

MASTERY TEST: UNDERSTANDING WORD PARTS

Complete the italicized word in each sentence by adding the correct word part. Use the meaning of the word part and the sentence context to determine the correct answer in each case.

inter- between   **de-** from, down   **dict-** say, tell, speak
sist- stand   **graph-** write   **post-** after, following
pend- hang, weigh   **vid-** see   **port-** carry
un- not, reverse

1. Sometimes, watching a music (. . . *eo*) _____ can ruin your own mental image of the song lyrics.

2. Following the birth of her baby, Jackie suffered from (. . . *natal*) _____ depression.

3. The English rock star who had been found guilty of drug possession was (*de . . . ed*) _____ by the Immigration Service.

4. A flat cord called a(n) (. . . *face*) _____ connects my computer to a printer.

5. One assignment in our English class is to write a (*bio . . . y*) _____ of another person in the class.

6. The psychic claimed to be (. . . *scended*) _____ from an Egyptian high priestess.

7. This year, I'm saving the (*pre . . . ions*) _____ that appeared in January's newspapers to see if any come true.

8. In the movie, the initialed (. . . *ant*) _____ around the boy's neck was the key to his true identity.

9. The (. . . *seasonable*) _____ warm weather has caused daffodils to bloom in January.

10. The (*in . . . ent*) _____ customer refused to step out of line at the complaint counter.

SCORE: Number correct (   ) x 10 = _____ %

MASTERY TEST: USING THE DICTIONARY

Part A. Use your dictionary to answer the following questions.

1. How many syllables are in the word *plausible*? _____

2. How many syllables are in the word *immaculate*?_____

3. How many syllables are in the word *fraternizing*?_____

4. Where is the primary accent in the word *exhalation*?_____

5. Where is the primary accent in the word *heterosexual*?_____

6. Where is the primary accent in the word *sociability*?_____

7. In the word *credence*, the first *e* is pronounced like
   a. long *e*.
   b. short *e*.
   c. schwa.
   d. short *i*.

8. In the word *maniacal*, the *i* is pronounced like
   a. schwa.
   b. short *i*.
   c. long *i*.
   d. long *e*.

9. In the word *emissary*, the *i* is pronounced like
   a. schwa.
   b. long *i*.
   c. short *i*.
   d. short *o*.

10. In the word *explicate*, the *i* is pronounced like
    a. schwa.
    b. long *i*.
    c. short *i*.
    d. long *e*.

Part B. There are five misspelled words in each of the following sentences. Cross out each misspelled word and write the correct spelling in the space provided.

11-15. Altho the lable carried no warning, the drug had serius side effects, such as migrane headaches.

_____ _____ _____ _____ _____

16-20. Because their were over fourty people waiting in line at the motor vehical office, I decided to wait until next Wedsday to get my motorcycle licence.

_____ _____ _____ _____ _____

> **SCORE:** Number correct ( ) x 5 = _____ %

81

MASTERY TEST: WORD PRONUNCIATION

Use slash marks to divide the following words into syllables.

General-Interest Words

1. ascertain

2. temporal

3. cognitive

4. obesity

5. interrogator

6. clandestine

7. reciprocate

8. verbatim

9. obfuscate

10. extemporize

11. subterfuge

12. tantamount

13. susurrant

14. multitudinous

15. asymmetric

Specialized Words

16. vascular

17. connate

18. interferon

19. columbite

20. laburnum

21. conjunctivitis

22. numismatic

23. safranine

24. circumduction

25. ventrodorsal

SCORE: Number correct (   ) x 4 = _____ %

MASTERY TEST: SPELLING IMPROVEMENT

Use the four spelling rules to spell the following words.

1. flip   + er   = _____

2. mighty   + ly   = _____

3. smile   + ing   = _____

4. bel _____ ve

5. occur   + ed   = _____

6. interfere   + ence   = _____

7. employ   + able   = _____

8. permit   + ing   = _____

9. arrive   + al   = _____

10. p _____ ce

11. threaten   + ed   = _____

12. empty   + ness   = _____

13. base   + ment   = _____

14. rel _____ f

15. copy   + ed   = _____

16. unforget   + able   = _____

17. compare   + ing   = _____

18. lovely   + er   = _____

19. athlete   + ic   = _____

20. regret   + ful   = _____

SCORE: Number correct (   ) x 5 = _____ %

MASTERY TEST: VOCABULARY DEVELOPMENT

Read each of the following sentences carefully. Then decide which of the choices provided comes closest in meaning to the italicized word. Circle the letter of your choice.

1. At the audition, the actors had to *improvise* a scene from an imaginary play.
   a. memorize   b. make up   c. understand   d. know   e. review

2. The Olympic runner *transcended* the difficulties that had been placed in his path and won a gold medal.
   a. remembered   b. surpassed   c. gave in to   d. enjoyed   e. added to

3. The professor gave the students who had cheated on the exam a *scathing* lecture on their lack of morals.
   a. harsh   b. boring   c. well-organized   d. pitiful   e. unclear

4. With her usual *candor*, the movie star admitted that she had once had a drug habit.
   a. humor   b. disgust   c. honesty   d. confusion   e. aggression

5. *Intermittent* bulletins throughout the day informed the nation about the status of the peace talks.
   a. overwhelming   b. long   c. untrue   d. friendly   e. occasional

6. Since my oral report was much too long, I decided to omit all *extraneous* information.
   a. basic   b. unessential   c. controversial   d. specific   e. statistical

7. Joanne is a *connoisseur* of fine food; she refuses to eat at McDonald's.
   a. cook   b. avoider   c. expert judge   d. overeater   e. reviewer

8. Some gods were thought to exert their powers in *malignant* ways unless won over by offerings or magic.
   a. unexpected   b. evil   c. beneficial   d. disgusting   e. mystical

9. Upon realizing my lab notebook was missing, I became *distraught* and began looking under everything in the apartment.
   a. panicky   b. amused   c. calm   d. dizzy   e. encouraged

10. Why there cannot be peace in the world is an *enigma* to many people.
    a. story   b. mystery   c. bore   d. challenge   e. fact

SCORE: Number correct (   ) x 10 = _____ %

MASTERY TEST: DEFINITIONS AND EXAMPLES

In the spaces provided, write the number of the sentence in each selection that contains a definition. Then write the number of the *first* sentence that provides an example of the definition.

A   [1]We have been talking about speech that is verbal, but human communication can take place by nonverbal means. [2]The term *symbolic speech* is used to refer to the communication of ideas and concepts by means of specific acts rather than words. [3]During the Vietnam War, for example, many persons wore either the peace symbol or an American flag on their clothing. [4]The peace symbol indicated that the wearer opposed the war; the American flag generally meant that the wearer supported the war.

B   [1]The desire to be with others is referred to as the need for *affiliation*. [2]This need seems to be greater when we are fearful or unsure of ourselves. [3]Nowhere is this more evident than in natural disasters. [4]Whether it's a volcano erupting, an earthquake, or a flood, pictures of the survivors almost always show them huddled together as if the mere physical presence of other people would avert further tragedy. [5]Even when the source of the fear proves to be unreal, those who share such fears band together to await the worst.

C   [1]A person's customs, beliefs, values, and technology are *interdependent*. [2]Changes in one area invariably affect other areas, sometimes throwing the entire system off balance. [3]For example, missionaries succeeded in converting large numbers of Madagascans to Christianity, with the result that theft, practically unknown in the pre-Christian days, became commonplace. [4]People stopped caring for their homes and villages because, as one researcher pointed out, "The fear of hell and the police are a poor substitute for the fear of ancestral ghosts who know everything and punished the evildoer with sickness on earth and exclusion from the ancestral village in the hereafter."

D   [1]Every product has a *life cycle,* a series of stages it goes through during the period it is available on the market. [2]This is a hard fact for some marketing executives to accept. [3]A product's life cycle is a bit like an insurance policy: we never know when it will mature, but its eventual end is certain. [4]The prediction in 1910 that horse-drawn wagons would pass out of daily life would have been met with laughter. [5]But that happened. [6]Today the life cycle of automobiles may seem endless, but already the use of cars has declined in large urban areas. [7]Pollution problems and fuel costs may hasten this reduced use (and production) of automobiles.

A   Definition: _____   Example: _____

B   Definition: _____   Example: _____

C   Definition: _____   Example: _____

D   Definition: _____   Example: _____

> **SCORE:** Number correct (   ) x 12.5 = _____ %

MASTERY TEST: ENUMERATIONS

Locate the enumerations in each of the following selections. Then number *1, 2, 3* . . . each of the items in the enumeration. You will find three items in A, three in B, and four in C.

A   A couple decide they will have children. When should they have them? Age is one consideration. The healthiest babies are born to mothers in their twenties. Babies born to women under 16 or over 40 are at greatest risk of being premature, stillborn, or having birth defects. Financial readiness is another factor. A couple should be financially secure enough to handle the cost of a new baby as well as the possible loss of income if the mother decides to give up her job. Emotional readiness is important, too. A husband-wife relationship needs to grow strong before it is ready to face the challenge of a third party. Potential parents must be mature enough to put the interests of another human being before their own.

B   For many old people, the special stresses of aging can make their last years a period of tremendous depression and anxiety. One source of stress is poverty. One out of every four Americans over sixty-five has an income below the poverty line; the rate is even higher for old people who live alone. Another source of stress is loneliness. Old people who no longer work miss the contacts provided by employment. Their children are on their own and may be living thousands of miles away. And at this age death takes a heavy toll—of friends, of relatives, of one's spouse. A final source of stress for the aged comes from the attitude of society itself. Because American culture is youth-oriented, we devalue the elderly. We invent euphemisms for them—"senior citizens," "golden-agers"—and tuck them away in hospitals and nursing homes. In a classic example of the self-fulfilling prophecy, people who are regarded as useless, self-involved, and befuddled often become just that.

C   A number of behaviors can lead to poor listening. First, people may act as though they are listening when they are, in reality, tuning the speaker out. Students, for example, often look directly at the professor and seem to be listening intently, but nothing is filtering through to their minds. Another behavior that results in poor listening is ignoring difficult material. Many people, for instance, avoid watching and listening to public television programs because they are "too hard to understand." If a speaker begins to talk or lecture about what a listener considers to be a difficult topic, the listener will ignore the rest of the talk. A third behavior that inhibits good listening skills is daydreaming. Every student is familiar with this situation: the professor is discussing psychology or history, but the student is fantasizing about tonight's party, summer vacation, or the student sitting close by. Finally, listeners may allow themselves to become distracted by other factors, such as the speaker's appearance or voice. Thinking about the speaker's accent or high-pitched voice or lime-green running shoes can prevent a listener from really hearing the speaker's message.

SCORE: Number correct (   ) x 10 = _____ %

MASTERY TEST: HEADINGS AND SUBHEADINGS

Part A.   Answer the three basic questions about the selection below.

Questions: What is aging? What are the results of aging? Why do we age?

Aging

Aging means that each person undergoes *senescence*, a gradual and inevitable decline in life's processes. Through this decline, a person's vulnerability to stress increases. Work performance may also be affected. A person may have less energy and may find some tasks harder. Aging occurs as the body's self-regulating mechanisms begin to break down, a process which causes problems with control of body temperature, hormonal secretions, blood-sugar level, and kidney function. There are also cumulative effects of stress due to chronic illness, radiation, smoking, overeating, and lack of exercise. Finally, there is a decline in the number of cells, a stiffening of the proteins called *collagen* and *elastin*, a limit to the number of times cells can reproduce, and an increase in cellular mutation.

Answers: _____

_____

_____

_____

_____

_____

Part B.   Using words such as *what*, *why*, *who*, *which*, *in what ways*, and *how*, write meaningful questions for each of the textbook heads that follow.

1. Teenage Suicides

   a. _____

   b. _____

2. Social Inequality in the United States

   a. _____

   b. _____

3. Publicity versus Advertising

   a. _____

   b. _____

   c. _____

SCORE: Number correct (   ) x 10 = _____ %

MASTERY TEST: SIGNAL WORDS

In the spaces provided, write the major signal words used in the following two selections. There are five major signal words in each selection.

A   Whatever the reason, IQ scores do predict success in school with some accuracy. Moreover, people with high IQ scores get into high-status occupations: doctors and lawyers tend to have high IQs; truck drivers and janitors tend not to have high IQs. But critics point out that this can be explained in various ways. For one thing, because people with higher IQs tend to do better in school, they stay in school longer; they get advanced degrees, which in turn open the door to high-status jobs. In addition, children from wealthy families are more likely to have the motivation and the money needed for graduate school and occupational training. Perhaps most important, they grow up in an environment that encourages academic success and rewards good performance on tests.

1. _____   3. _____   5. _____

2. _____   4. _____

B   An important negative consequence of this emphasis on sports is that the rewards from the school, community, and peer group for success in sports are a deterrent to academic achievement. Coleman found, for example, that in response to the question, "How would you most like to be remembered here at high school?" 44 percent wished to be remembered as an athletic star, while only 31 percent wanted to be remembered as a brilliant student. On the other hand, three-fourths of the parents of these boys wanted their boys to be remembered as brilliant students. Coleman determined that people with the greatest talent divert their energies away from scholarship to athletics, where the rewards are. Adolescents who are labeled "scholars" are, therefore, not necessarily those with the highest intelligence: they are only the ones who are willing to work hard at a relatively unrewarding activity. Thus, with the blessing of the community and the school authorities, the schools engage in activities that actually work against the objectives of the school.

1. _____   3. _____   5. _____

2. _____   4. _____

SCORE: Number correct (   ) x 10 = _____ %

MASTERY TEST: MAIN IDEA

Locate and underline the main idea sentence in each of the selections that follow. Then, in the space provided, write the number of the main idea sentence.

A   [1]A campaign for clean inner air is being waged by nonsmokers in private homes and public places. [2]Some colleges have banned smoking in classrooms. [3]Some people have posted signs in their homes: "Thank you for not smoking" or "If you must smoke, don't exhale." [4]One restaurant started with a thirty-five-seat nonsmoking section and now reports that half the eight hundred diners served daily are requesting "no smoking" space. [5]A beautician who set up nonsmoking days has found them to be very popular with patrons. [6]And some entertainers ask nightclubbers to stop smoking during their acts.

B   [1]The psychological costs of sexism to women have received a great deal of attention in recent years, but the strains placed on men have been neglected. [2]In fact, however, the role traditionally played by men is a very stressful and demanding one, and there is no shortage of hard data to bear this out. [3]Men are five times more likely than women to commit suicide. [4]They are three times more likely to suffer from severe mental disorders. [5]They are disproportionately likely to suffer from all stress-related illnesses, such as ulcers, asthma, hypertension, and heart disease. [6]They are six times more likely than women to become alcoholics, and the overwhelming majority of narcotics addicts are male. [7]Men are far more frequently involved in acts of violence; they are arrested eight times as often for murder as women, and are arrested for 88 percent of violent crimes.

C.   [1]The average Native American has only eight years of schooling. [2]Unemployment generally ranges between 45 and 55 percent, but reaches 80 percent in some areas and seasons. [3]Almost half of employed Native Americans who live on the reservations work in some capacity for government agencies. [4]About a third of the Native American population lives below the poverty line, and many, if not most, reservation dwellings are substandard: thousands of people are living in unheated log houses, tar-paper shacks, old tents, caves, and even abandoned automobile bodies. [5]The life expectancy of the average Native American is ten years below that of the nation as a whole. [6]The suicide rate is double the national average, and the alcoholism rate is at least five times as high. [7]All in all, the current social and economic position of the Native American is probably worse than that of any other minority group in the United States.

D.   [1]A commercial product's bundle of satisfaction includes not only its tangible features but also its intangible characteristics, such as store image, guarantees, and brand names. [2]Even so, the product's price is often the overriding ingredient that leads to an exchange. [3]Many consumers, for instance, derive satisfaction from getting a product at a "good price"; they like to get, say, five double-edged razor blades for only 99 cents when the regular price is $1.49. [4]Some people just love a "bargain"; the word *sale* alone often stimulates exchange. [5]And at the other end of the scale, some consumers gain satisfaction from acquiring an expensive product. [6]There is a definite "snob appeal" at work when a Rolls-Royce can sell for more than $40,000—surely more than one need pay for transportation.

A _____   B _____   C _____   D _____

> **SCORE:** Number correct (   ) x 25 = _____ %

MASTERY TEST: OUTLINING I

Major and minor ideas are mixed together in the list below. Put the ideas into logical order by filling in the outline that follows the list. The outline is partially completed.

Places to eat
Steel mill
Automobile plant
Pancake house
Buildings
Chinese restaurant
Concert hall
Places that provide
  entertainment

Gymnasium
Ice skating rink
Offices
Movie theater
Insurance office
Steak house
Cafeteria
Real estate office

Fast food restaurant
Sports facility
Specialty restaurant
Places to work
Knitting mill
Internal Revenue office
Factories

(Title) _____

  I. _____
     A. _Factories_ _____
        1. _____
        2. _____
        3. _____
     B. _____
        1. _____
        2. _____
        3. _____

 II. _____
     A. _Movie theater_ _____
     B. _____
     C. _____
        1. _____
        2. _____

III. _____
     A. _____
     B. _____
     C. _Specialty restaurant_ _____
        1. _____
        2. _____
        3. _____

SCORE: Number correct (___) x 5 = _____ %

90

MASTERY TEST: OUTLINING II

Read the following selection and then complete the outline that follows it.

Both labor and management have weapons to use in settling a conflict, and we shall examine those weapons now. The *strike* remains the most potent weapon that labor can use to force management to accept its point of view. Strikes can take various forms: walkouts, sit-down strikes, sympathy strikes, and wildcat strikes. Labor also has other weapons. *Picketing* is designed to inform the public of grievances and to encourage nonstriking workers to leave their jobs. Another labor weapon is *boycotts*. *Primary boycotts* attempt to induce union members and the general public not to buy products of firms against which they have complaints. *Secondary boycotts* attempt to put economic pressure on employers by getting other industries not to use or handle their products.

Many of the historic weapons of management to combat union activity have been outlawed. These now-illegal weapons included *yellow-dog contracts* and *blacklisting* of employees who were union organizers. The legal means that remain for management to use in time of strikes or other labor conflicts include *lockouts*, which keep workers from entering the business premises so that management can either operate the plant with other workers or shut it down. Management also uses *strikebreakers*, hiring other workers to perform the work of striking workers. Other management weapons are *strike insurance* and a united organization of managements.

(Title) _____

I. _____

   A. _____

      1. _____

      2. _____

      3. _____

      4. _____

   B. _____

   C. _____

      1. _____

      2. _____

II. _____

   A. _____

      1. _____

      2. _____

   B. _____

      1. _____

      2. _____

      3. _____

      4. _____

SCORE: Number correct ( ) x 5 = _____ %

MASTERY TEST: OUTLINING III

Sometimes it helps to take study notes in the form of highly visual outlines. Complete the five missing items in the visual outline provided for the following passage.

In ordinary speech, the word "culture" is often used to refer to sophisticated tastes in art, literature, or music. The sociological use of the term is much wider, for it includes the entire way of life of a society. In this sense, everyone who participates in society is "cultured." To the sociologist, *culture consists of all the shared products of human society*. These products are of two basic kinds, material and nonmaterial. *Material culture* consists of all the manufactured products that human beings create and give meaning to; examples are wheels, clothing, books, spacecraft, totem poles. *Nonmaterial culture* consists of the words people use, the ideas they hold, and the habits they follow. In the game of baseball, for instance, the gloves and bats are elements of material culture; the rules of the games, the skills of the players, and the traditional behavior of players and spectators are all parts of nonmaterial culture.

CULTURE

```
┌─────────────────────────────────────────────────┐
│ Culture—                                         │
│                                                  │
│                                                  │
│                                                  │
│                                                  │
└─────────────────────────────────────────────────┘
              TWO KINDS OF CULTURE

┌──────────────────────┐      ┌──────────────────────┐
│ Material culture—     │      │ Nonmaterial culture—  │
│                      │      │                      │
│                      │      │                      │
│ Ex—                  │      │ Ex—                  │
│                      │      │                      │
└──────────────────────┘      └──────────────────────┘
```

SCORE: Number correct (   ) x 20 = _____ %

MASTERY TEST: SUMMARIZING

Circle the letter of the title that best summarizes each selection. Remember that the title should be as specific and descriptive as possible while at the same time accounting for all the material in the selection.

A   It is obvious to college students that the principal purpose of their written work in school is to demonstrate knowledge and ability to an instructor. Yet many people forget this purpose when they start writing reports, letters, or memorandums in business. You cannot afford to forget how important your writing is to your personal success. Numerous studies have shown that business people typically rank facility in business communication at or near the top of any list of abilities needed for optimum business performance. But despite this united appeal for skill in this area, we are being told that among average high school graduates, writing performance is deteriorating at an alarming rate. Such an indictment is admittedly frightening; yet interpreted from a personal standpoint, it supports the idea that the employee who can write well will have a significant edge in promotability over the many who cannot.

a. The Importance of Writing Skills in Business
b. Declining Writing Performance in High Schools
c. Getting an Edge over the Competition
d. Business Communications Skills

B   People often use the threat of punishment to prevent unwanted behavior in others. For example, judges who want to stop a particular kind of crime may use stiff penalties to deter the criminal. Are these tactics likely to be effective? It appears that they are not. Research shows that, when a person is considering committing a crime, he or she first considers the reward a successful crime would bring. Only secondarily does the person consider the punishment involved. Further, if penalties are raised, certain groups may resent what they consider to be unjust treatment and may increase their unlawfulness. For example, the U.S. Army found that unlawful acts increased when punishments were stricter, apparently because people resented the harsh treatment. Finally, juries tend to be lenient toward a defendant if the punishment for the crime is high. Thus, using strong punishment—such as the death penalty—to stop crime would not appear to be very effective. More promising approaches might be to increase rewards for positive behavior or decrease the reward for criminal activity.

a. Capital Punishment
b. Criminals and Their Motivations
c. The Ineffectiveness of Punishment in Preventing Crime
d. The Judicial System and Penalties for Criminals

SCORE: Number correct (   ) x 50 = _____ %

MASTERY TEST: APPLYING SEVERAL READING SKILLS I

Read the passage below and then answer the questions that follow. Several reading skills are involved: identifying vocabulary in context; summarizing a selection in a several-word title; finding the main idea; identifying a key detail; and drawing a conclusion.

For the past twenty years, poll takers have told us that the vast majority of Americans report that they are "satisfied" or "very satisfied" with their jobs. But when the surveys pose a slightly different question—"If you had it to do over again, would you choose the same line of work?"—60 percent of working Americans say they would choose another occupation. This seems to tell us that Americans feel that they are supposed to like their jobs, but, in reality, they don't. Most of us are stuck in jobs we'd prefer not to have. And some of us actually hate what we do.

How does this happen in a land where citizens are presumably free to do, and become, anything they want? First of all, some of us didn't deliberately choose our jobs but simply fell into them. Later, there was never time to find out what we really wanted to do. Another reason people dislike their jobs is the result of a change in the American economy. A hundred years ago, most Americans worked for themselves on farms or in small stores and workshops. Now, less than 10 percent of us are self-employed. Many of us work as cogs in the wheels of giant corporations. We don't make a finished product with our own hands, and we feel that we are totally replaceable parts in the machine. Social scientists say that the happiest workers are the ones who are their own bosses— business owners, executives, and professionals. Working for a big company often results in a sense of powerlessness and *malaise*. Finally, being a member of the baby-boom generation increases the chances of job dissatisfaction. In the scramble for careers among the members of this large population "bulge," many people are losing out in the competition. These people may never achieve the standard of living their parents achieved, or go as far up the ladder of success as they had hoped. The result is bitterness, disillusionment, and a feeling of being trapped in a "nowhere" job.

1. The word *malaise* means
   a. depression.
   b. fulfillment.
   c. contentment.
   d. significance.

2. What is the best title for this selection?
   a. Job Satisfaction
   b. Why People Hate Their Jobs
   c. Nowhere Jobs
   d. A Change in the Workplace

3. Which sentence best expresses the main idea of the selection?
   a. Job burnout is a growing problem.
   b. Large companies provide many benefits to workers.
   c. Workers are unhappy because they no longer work with their hands.
   d. There are several reasons why workers are unhappy with their jobs.

4. According to the passage, the majority of Americans
   a. would choose another occupation if they could begin again.
   b. are self-employed.
   c. feel that they are supposed to dislike their jobs.
   d. work in factories.

5. The author implies that
   a. job dissatisfaction is a sign of laziness.
   b. the baby-boomers despise their parents.
   c. polls can be misleading.
   d. working for a corporation is very satisfying.

SCORE: Number correct (   ) x 20 = _____ %

MASTERY TEST: APPLYING SEVERAL READING SKILLS II

Read the passage below and then answer the questions that follow. Several reading skills are involved: identifying vocabulary in context; summarizing a selection in a several-word title; finding the main idea; identifying a key detail; and drawing a conclusion.

Some hospital doctors send an assistant rather than come themselves to talk with patients after an operation. Other patients wait in vain for visits from doctors who simply forget to come. When some doctors come to examine a patient in a semiprivate room or in a ward, they don't even take the seconds needed to draw the privacy curtains around the bed. Some doctors are so *callous* that they ask intimate questions in front of visitors. For example, as my boss sat in a chair nearby, I was asked by my doctor when I had my last menstrual period. And there are doctors who, without getting the patient's permission, bring classes of medical students who congregate around the patient's bed. They then discuss the patient's case as if she or he were a medical specimen or a corpse lying there not hearing a word being said.

Some people say that because hospitals are so overcrowded with patients, doctors must use their time as efficiently as possible. Others say that doctors are so busy making money that they don't want to take time to spend with patients. But no matter how busy doctors are, it is important for them to show human sensitivity.

1. The word *callous* means
    a. understanding.
    b. hardened.
    c. hurried.
    d. curious.

2. Which is the most accurate title for this selection?
    a. Common Courtesy
    b. Malpractitioners
    c. Bad Manners
    d. Insensitive Doctors

3. Which statement best expresses the main idea of the passage?
    a. Doctors are interested in efficiency.
    b. The writer's experience with her doctor was not unusual.
    c. Some doctors are too busy.
    d. Some doctors are insensitive.

4. *True or false?* _____ The writer's doctor did not even come into her room.

5. A patient whose case is being objectively discussed by a doctor and medical students is likely to feel
    a. uncomfortable.
    b. flattered.
    c. bored.
    d. restless.

SCORE: Number correct (   ) x 20 = _____ %

MASTERY TEST: APPLYING SEVERAL READING SKILLS III

Read the passage below and then answer the questions that follow.

A three-year-old Massachusetts boy is kidnapped. His captor moves him from state to state, beats him, and half-starves him. The boy's mother spends six years trying to locate her son. Perhaps the worst part of this terrible story is the kidnapper's identity: he is the boy's father. In New Jersey, a divorced woman is ordered by the court to hand over her daughter to the child's father for the Christmas holidays. The mother does not realize at the time that she will never see her daughter again—the father will kidnap her.

Parental kidnapping—snatching a child from a parent who has legal custody—is a growing problem linked to the climbing divorce rate. In the overwhelming majority of divorce cases, mothers are granted custody; therefore, fathers are usually the ones who kidnap their own children. The number of cases of parental kidnapping has soared to over 100,000 per year. The American Bar Association estimates that seven out of ten kidnapped children will never see the other parent again.

The reasons why a parent kidnaps a child are usually *not* rooted in feelings of love and loneliness for a child. Instead, parents kidnap children because they are angry and resentful. They want to "get back" at an ex-spouse. Often, the kidnappers take out their hostile feelings on the child. Many such parents, for instance, physically abuse the children once they have them. Sometimes, horribly, the child is murdered. Even if the children are not physically injured, they are emotionally damaged by being uprooted from family and friends and being moved from state to state in a *clandestine* lifestyle.

The parents of abducted children suffer as well. The agony of not knowing where the child is or how the child is being treated is constant. Some parents spend a great deal of time and money in a useless attempt to try to track down the child. The frustration involved leaves these parents embittered and despairing. Clearly, the problem of parental kidnapping is a national tragedy. Every day some child becomes the prize in a game of tug-of-war between parents, a dangerous game that scars the players for life.

1. The word *clandestine* means
   a. secretive.
   b. showy.
   c. contented.
   d. insulting.

2. An appropriate title for this selection would be:
   a. A Starving Child
   b. Parents and Children
   c. Parental Kidnapping
   d. The Drawbacks of Divorce

3. The main idea of the selection is that
   a. both parents and children suffer when a child is kidnapped.
   b. divorced spouses will do terrible things to each other.
   c. the custody laws are unfair.
   d. kidnapped children are treated well.

4. According to the passage, the main reason why parents kidnap their children is
   a. loneliness and despair.
   b. love and concern.
   c. resentment and anger.
   d. excitement and optimism.

5. One can conclude from the passage that
   a. divorced spouses need to work out better custody arrangements.
   b. children of divorce will grow to hate their parents.
   c. most children who are kidnapped by one parent get returned.
   d. the number of child kidnappings will continue to rise along with the divorce rate.

SCORE: Number correct ( ) x 20 = _____ %

MASTERY TEST: READING A TABLE

Answer the questions about the table that follows.

Numbers of Deaths among Young Adults (15- to 24-year-olds)

Causes of Death	Females		Males	
	White	Other	White	Other
Accidents	4517	585	16986	2228
Cancer	885	146	1402	226
Homicide	613	518	1850	2057
Suicide	839	122	3354	432
Heart Diseases	248	134	489	201

(Source: National Center for Health Statistics)

1. What is the leading cause of death for all young adults?

   _____

2. How many nonwhite females committed suicide during the year these statistics were compiled? _____

3. Among all the groups, which is most threatened by cancer? _____

4. Which group is more likely to die from heart disease—white females or white males?

   _____

5. What is the source for all the statistics shown?

   _____

SCORE: Number correct ( ) x 20 = _____ %

97

MASTERY TEST: STUDYING MATH AND SCIENCE; MAKING INFERENCES; CONNECTING READING AND WRITING

Some of the questions that follow are true-false or multiple-choice questions, and some require you to write short answers.

1. Math and science courses are difficult for many students because these subjects
   a. require certain basic skills a student may have forgotten (or never mastered).
   b. have their own vocabularies, rules, and formulas.
   c. demand a great deal of hard work.
   d. all of the above.

2. In math and science, knowledge is cumulative (each lesson builds on the ones before it). Therefore, students in these courses should
   a. attend every class.
   b. keep up to date with the assignments.
   c. get extra help with any concept or problem they don't understand.
   d. all of the above.

3. One study technique that works well in math and science is
   a. catchwords.   c. writing down enumerations.
   b. flashcards.   d. all of the above.

4. *True or false?* _____ Note-taking is not as important in a math class as it is in other subjects.

5. With a science textbook, it is important to study the _____ as well as the written explanations.

6. In a piece of literature, *theme* refers to the
   a. overall idea that the author is presenting.
   b. ending of the story.
   c. climax of the story.
   d. major conflict on which the story is based.

7. *True or false?* _____ Writers of factual material usually state directly what they mean; writers of fiction often show what they mean.

8. In making inferences, it's important to
   a. know a good deal about the author's background.
   b. have a good vocabulary.
   c. "read between the lines."
   d. have studied in advance the author's beliefs.

9. *True or false?* _____ Reading poetry requires more inferences than other kinds of literature.

10. One similarity between reading and writing is that both
   a. demand a large vocabulary.
   b. are processes that involve several steps.
   c. require a student to make inferences.
   d. all of the above.

> **SCORE:** Number correct (   ) x 10 = _____ %

ANSWERS TO THE THIRTY ADDITIONAL MASTERY TESTS

Motivational Skills

1. an inner commitment to doing the work
2. b. playing games.
3. Avoidance tactics include the following: "I can't do it." "I'm too busy." "I'm too tired." "I'll do it later." "I'm bored with the subject." "I'm here, and that's what counts."
4. b. talk to someone about it.
5. a. on the first day
6. study
7. d. all of the above.
8. d. surviving.
9. d. has closed herself off from growth.
10. nobody

Taking Classroom Notes

1. c
2. False
3. d
4. dg (*or* def. grat.)
5. b
6. d
7. False
8. d
9. a
10. c

Time Control and Concentration

1. c
2. d
3. True
4. a
5. False
6. reward yourself.
7. c
8. False
9. b
10. d

The PRWR Study Method

1. Recite.
2. True
3. c
4. False
5. a
6. c
7. d
8. True
9. d
10. recall

Using PRWR

1. letters
2. *For example:* FEMP
3. letter
4. *For example:* **Ed sells rabbits.**
5. (1) intimacy
6. (2) generativity
7. (3) integrity
8. *For example:* **Ice got inside.**

Taking Textbook Study Notes

1-4. *Stages in Unemployment:* (1) Shock, relief, and relaxation
                                           (2) Effort to find a new job
                                           (3) Loss of self-esteem; high levels of self-doubt and anxiety
                                           (4) Resignation and withdrawal

5. *Reactions to the fourth stage:* (1) Conscious decision to change careers; search for other sources of self-esteem

Building a Powerful Memory

1. b
2. False
3. b
4. d
5. c
6. spread out
7. c
8. True
9. Answers will vary. Examples: HOMES, HEMOS
10. Answers will vary. Example: Larry loves cooked turnips.

Taking Objective Exams

1. False—D
2. c—B
3. True—C
4. d—A
5. False—D
6. c—B
7. True—C
8. d—A

Taking Objective and Essay Exams

1. _____

    Langan, John *(upside down)*

    (printed)

2. _____

    Langan, John

    (written)

3. c. Compare
4. d. Trace
5. easiest
6. time
7. False
8. True
9. d. Prepare several "cram sheets" full of important ideas to study.
10. d. try to rephrase difficult questions in your own words.

Using the Library and the Internet

1. b
2. subject
3. d
4. True
5. "Are Human Experiments Too Dangerous?"
6. S. Begley and D. Foote
7. Pages 38 to 42
8. August 6, 2001
9. b
10. True

Writing a Research Paper

1. True
2. b
3. point
4. c
5. c

6. False
7. b
8. thesis
9. True
10. a

Understanding Word Parts

1. video
2. postnatal
3. deported
4. interface
5. biography

6. descended
7. predictions
8. pendant
9. unseasonable
10. insistent

Using the Dictionary

1. three
2. four
3. four
4. exhaLAtion
5. heteroSEXual

6. sociaBILity
7. a. long *e*
8. c. long *i*
9. a. schwa
10. c. short *i*

11-15. Although. . . label. . . carried. . . serious. . . migraine
16-20. there. . . forty. . . vehicle. . . Wednesday. . . license

Word Pronunciation

1. as/cer/tain
2. tem/po/ral
3. cog/ni/tive
4. o/be/si/ty
5. in/ter/ro/ga/tor
6. clan/des/tine
7. re/cip/ro/cate
8. ver/ba/tim
9. ob/fus/cate
10. ex/tem/po/rize
11. sub/ter/fuge
12. tan/ta/mount
13. su/sur/rant
14. mul/ti/tu/di/nous
15. a/sym/met/ric

16. vas/cu/lar
17. con/nate
18. in/ter/fer/on
19. co/lum/bite
20. la/bur/num
21. con/junc/ti/vi/tis
22. nu/mis/ma/tic
23. saf/ra/nine
24. cir/cum/duc/tion
25. ven/tro/dor/sal

Spelling Improvement

1. flipper
2. mightily
3. smiling
4. believe
5. occurred
6. interference
7. employable
8. permitting
9. arrival
10. piece
11. threatened
12. emptiness
13. basement
14. relief
15. copied
16. unforgettable
17. comparing
18. lovelier
19. athletic
20. regretful

Vocabulary Development

1. b. make up
2. b. surpassed
3. a. harsh
4. c. honesty
5. e. occasional
6. b. unessential
7. c. expert judge
8. b. evil
9. a. panicky
10. b. mystery

Definitions and Examples

A	Definition: 2	Example: 3	
B	Definition: 1	Example: 4	
C	Definition: 2	Example: 3	
D	Definition: 1	Example: 4	

Enumerations

A Factors in Deciding When to Have Children
    1. Age
    2. Financial readiness
    3. Emotional readiness

B Stresses of Aging
    1. Poverty
    2. Loneliness
    3. Society's attitude

C Behaviors Leading to Poor Listening
    1. Tuning the speaker out
    2. Ignoring difficult material
    3. Daydreaming
    4. Becoming distracted by other factors

Headings and Subheadings

A   1. *What is aging?* Aging occurs when a person undergoes *senescence*, a gradual and inevitable decline in life's processes.

2. *What are the results of aging?* Aging results in increased vulnerability to stress and poor work performance due to loss of energy.

3. *Why do we age?* The body's self-regulating mechanisms begin to break down, the cumulative effects of lifelong stresses are felt, the number of cells declines, proteins stiffen, and cells reproduce less and mutate more.

B   *Note:* Answers may vary; here are some possible questions for each topic. Students should create two questions each for "Teenage Suicides" and "Social Inequality in the United States" and three questions for "Publicity versus Advertising."

1. Why do teenagers commit suicide?
   Which teenagers commit suicide?
   How many teenagers commit suicide?
   What can be done to stop teenage suicides?

2. What is social inequality?
   How does social inequality affect Americans?
   In what ways are Americans unequal?
   What are some causes of social inequality?

3. What is publicity?
   What is advertising?
   How does publicity differ from advertising?
   Is one more effective than the other?

Signal Words

A   1. Moreover
     2. But
     3. For one thing
     4. In addition
     5. most important

B   1. important
     2. for example
     3. On the other hand
     4. therefore
     5. Thus

Main Idea

A   1
B   2

C   7
D   2

Outlining I

Note: Sequence of subitems may vary.

Buildings
  I. Places to work
    A. Factories
      1. Steel mill
      2. Automobile plant
      3. Knitting mill
    B. Offices
      1. Insurance office
      2. Internal Revenue office
      3. Real estate office
  II. Places that provide entertainment
    A. Movie theater
    B. Concert hall
    C. Sports facility
      1. Gymnasium
      2. Ice skating rink
  III. Places to eat
    A. Cafeteria
    B. Fast-food restaurant
    C. Specialty restaurant
      1. Steak house
      2. Chinese restaurant
      3. Pancake house

Outlining II

Weapons in Settling a Conflict
  I. Labor's weapons
    A. Strike
      1. Walkouts
      2. Sitdown
      3. Sympathy
      4. Wildcat
    B. Picketing
    C. Boycotts
      1. Primary
      2. Secondary
  II. Management's weapons
    A. Illegal
      1. Yellow-dog contracts
      2. Blacklisting of employees
    B. Legal
      1. Lockouts
      2. Strikebreakers
      3. Strike insurance
      4. United organization of managements

Outlining III

Culture—all the shared products of human society.

Material culture—all the manufactured products that human beings create and give meaning to.
   Ex—Wheels, clothing, books. *(Other examples are possible.)*
Nonmaterial culture—the words people use, the ideas they hold, and the habits they follow.
   Ex—rules of the game in baseball. *(Other examples are possible.)*

Summarizing

A   a. The Importance of Writing Skills in Business
B   c. The Ineffectiveness of Punishment in Preventing Crime

Applying Several Reading Skills I

1. a. depression.
2. b. Why People Hate Their Jobs
3. d. There are several reasons why workers are unhappy with their jobs.
4. a. would choose another occupation if they could begin again.
5. c. Polls can be misleading.

Applying Several Reading Skills II

1. b. hardened.
2. d. Insensitive Doctors
3. d. Some doctors are insensitive.
4. False
5. a. uncomfortable.

Applying Several Reading Skills III

1. a. secretive.
2. c. Parental Kidnapping
3. a. both parents and children suffer when a child is kidnapped.
4. c. resentment and anger.
5. d. the number of child kidnappings will continue to rise along with the divorce rate.

Reading a Table

1. Accidents
2. 122
3. White males
4. White males
5. National Center for Health Statistics

Studying Math and Science; Making Inferences; Connecting Reading and Writing

1. d
2. d
3. d
4. False
5. visual material *or* charts and diagrams

6. a
7. True
8. c
9. True
10. b